MAKING DRIED FLOWER ARRANGEMENTS

MAKING DRIED
FLOWER ARRANGEMENTS

Barbara Coates

Kangaroo Press

Dedicated to
my greatest supporter
—my beloved husband David

Acknowledgments

'Oasis' is the registered trademark of the Smithers-Oasis Company, Adelaide.
'Parafilm' is made by Floral Products Co., Greenwich, Connecticut, USA.

Drawings by Barbara Coates and Kim Maciuk.
Arrangements by Barbara Coates.
Fridge magnet and terracotta pot door hanger by Dorothy Clifton.
Photography by Bruce Devine of Murwillumbah and
Photo-Link of South Tweed Heads.

First published in 1994 by Kangaroo Press Pty Ltd
3 Whitehall Road Kenthurst NSW 2156 Australia
P.O. Box 6125 Dural Delivery Centre NSW 2158
Typeset by G.T. Setters Pty Limited
Printed in Hong Kong through Colorcraft Ltd

ISBN 0 86417 579 5

CONTENTS

INTRODUCTION

What could be more rewarding for a keen gardener than to be able to preserve the flowers and foliages on which much pleasurable effort has been expended?

The art of drying flowers and foliages, which has long been practised, provides a logical answer in today's rushed society for those who wish to decorate their homes with low maintenance floral arrangements. Not everyone can remember to top up water levels daily in fresh floral displays. And there is something special about the rustic charm dried flowers and foliages bring to a room.

The mere techniques employed to dry flowers and foliages can in themselves be rewarding for the hobbyist. Timing plays a large part and the skills involved can give a strong sense of personal satisfaction when the task has been well done. Today's uses for dried flowers and foliages are only limited by the imagination. One need not be restricted to producing only bowl, vase or basket arrangements, beautiful though they may be—novelty gift items such as decorated wall brooms, coathangers and kitchen spice ropes all hold visual appeal.

A big plus is that dried flowers and foliages are so easy to look after. Just keep them out of direct sunlight to prevent colours fading and keep them clean by blowing the dust away with the nozzle of a vacuum cleaner. Your arrangements should keep their looks for at least two years.

Probably the most rewarding of all dried flower arrangements for the busy person are those fresh flower arrangements which can be left to dry on their own. This way the beauty of living flowers can be enjoyed first and then combined with the delight of seeing the arrangements turn into something everlasting.

The commercial flower grower should also find a selling bonus when considering dried flowers and foliages. Fresh flower losses can mount up so growing flowers which can be dried can provide a back up to sales.

Whatever your reason, interest in dried flowers and foliages is increasing. This book covers the basic principles of flower arranging, presents seventeen examples of finished arrangements with detailed instructions, and ends with an informative section on how best to dry flowers, which includes extensive illustrated listings of flowers and foliages best suited to the various drying techniques.

1 BASIC TECHNIQUES

Stem wiring

Single-leg mount wiring

This technique is used in this book to wire the clusters of flowers forming the flower circle used as the hat decoration for the bride (page 41). It is commonly used with flowers which have delicate stems or no subtantial base or calyx or, as in this case, where natural stems are inconvenient.

Technique
Make a small hook at one end of an 0.46 mm gauge wire. Cut chosen flowers from branches, leaving 2.5 cm stems. Pieces of foliage can also be added. Place clustered stalks against the hook so they are supported by it.

Wind the wire just below the hook, twice around the stem and base of the hook.

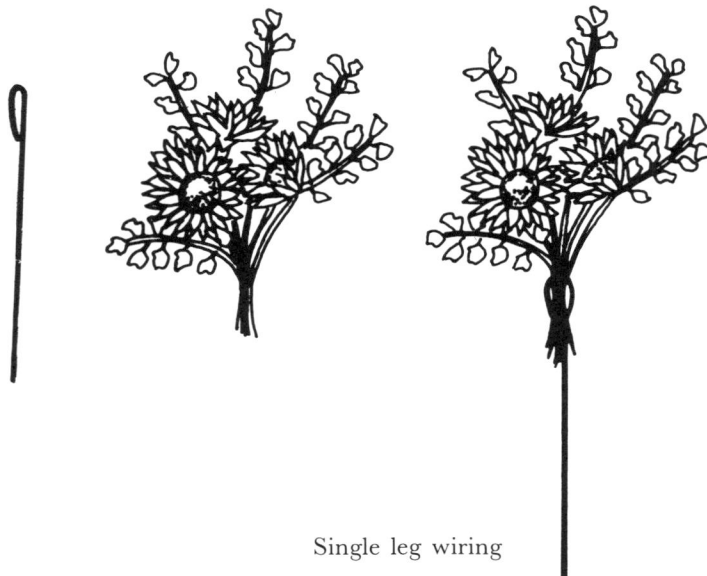

Double-leg mount wiring

This method can be used to group a variety of flowers and foliages together or for grouping of one species only where flower stems are broken or too fragile to be placed directly into base material such as Oasis foam.

Technique
Cut flower stalks 2.5 cm long. Using 0.71 gauge wire, almost centre the wire behind the stems. Bring the longer of the two ends up and wind it twice around the stems and other wire, then bend it down to the side, matching the other end of the wire for length. Parafilm.

Single leg wiring

Double leg wiring

Parafilming

Covering wired stems with tape not only hides the ugliness of bare wire but helps to hold the wired flowers and leaves in position. 'Parafilm' is a stretchable tape which clings to itself. When covering stems, the idea is to stretch this tape to a fine skin which should become barely discernable. It should not be treated as a bandage.

Technique
Hold the wired stem between thumb and index finger just below the flower head. Hold the end of the Parafilm in the opposite hand. Place the tape against the base of the flower where the wiring starts. Wind the tape around the flower base and subsequently over itself once, stretching the tape thinly as you do so. Don't be too concerned if the tape snaps as you can stick it back on itself and start again.

Use the thumb and index finger of the hand holding the stem to begin a twisting motion. That is, the stem will be twirled, almost in the one position, while the opposite hand will start stretching and pulling down on the tape. With practice you will find a natural rhythm occurring between the two hands. The hand pulling down on the tape will be doing the most moving.

When the stem is covered with tape, run your hand smoothly down the wire to give a finish to the tape.

Florist's bows

Flat looped bow

Reverse these instructions if you are left-handed. The bow described here is a flat 4-looped bow with 5 cm (2'') loops. Following the same principles you can make bows with 6 or 8 loops, tiny loops, flat loops—whatever you want.

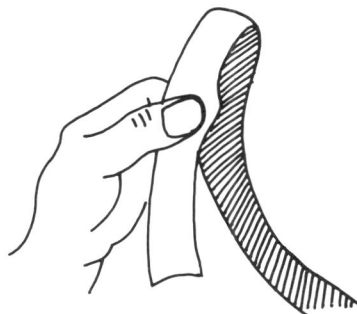

Hold the ribbon 5 cm (2'') from one end between your thumb and index finger. Make a loop 5 cm (2'') long by placing the long part of the ribbon behind the ribbon already held between your thumb and index finger.

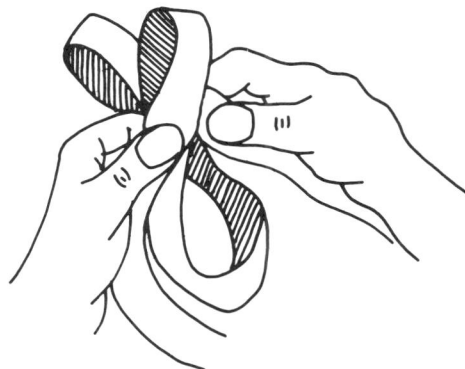

The long piece of ribbon is now used to form your next loop. Take the long piece of ribbon in your right hand and forming a loop the same size as the previous one, fold the long piece of ribbon up and behind and slightly to the left of your original loop. Look at the second diagram. You now have one loop on either side of your hand. Your right hand holding the ribbon shows you how it is going to be pushed to the left of the first loop to form the third loop.

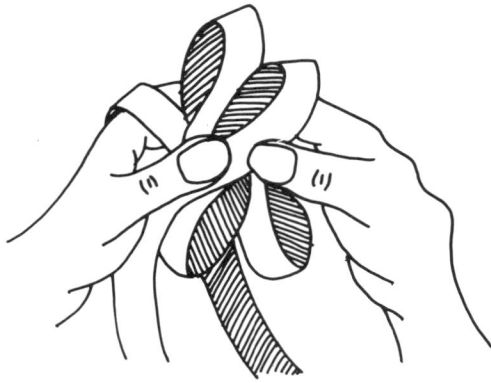

Now form the third loop, which will also measure 5 cm (2''). After doing this the long piece of ribbon is now on the opposite side of the bow, slightly to the right of loop two. This will be used to form the fourth loop.

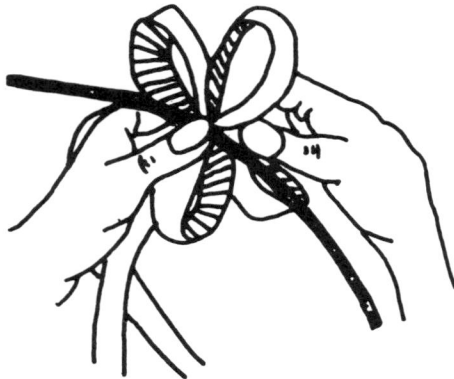

With your free hand pick up a 23 cm (9'') length of wire, 0.71 mm gauge. Slip the wire underneath your thumb, centering it over the centre of your bow.

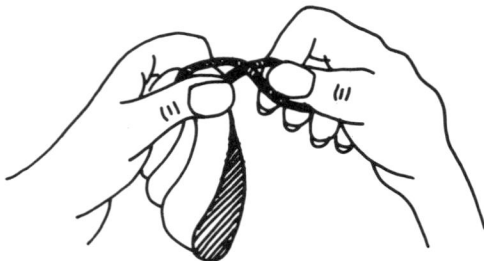

Put your free hand up behind the bow, clasping both ends of the wire (which is still over the bow). Pull both ends of the wire down, twisting the wire tight from behind as you do so. A pair of pliers come in handy at this point as they can tighten the wire more firmly than fingers. The tighter the wire the more secure the loops

and the more the loops stand out. You can now arrange and straighten any droopy loops. Cut the ribbon end 5 cm (2'') long to match the first. Cut ribbon ends on a slant.

Fancy flower bow

This is a spectacular, highly decorative bow used at the base of hand posies and sheaves. Reverse instructions if left handed.

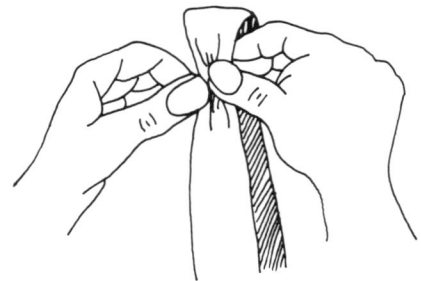

Allow 2 m (80'') of tear ribbon. Leave the ribbon at its original width. Hold the ribbon 7.5 cm (3'') from one end, between the thumb and index finger of your left hand, pinching the ribbon in towards the centre.

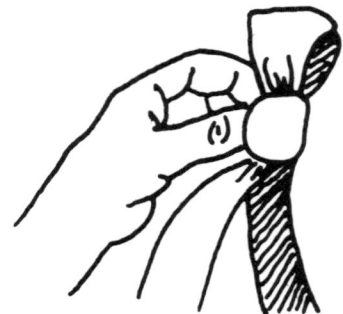

Bring the long end of the ribbon over the top of your thumb, so that your thumb is sitting inside a loop approximately 2.5 cm (1'') in diameter. The long end of the ribbon is behind the loop, held between your thumb and index finger.

Make a loop 7.5 cm (3'') long, then with the long piece of ribbon make another loop opposite the first loop.

Make another loop 7.5 cm (3'') in length, pinching it in at the centre. As you make each loop, you may find it easier to move the bow from one hand to the other so that each loop you make can be positioned appropriately.

Make at least four loops, pinching each one in at the centre.

When you have enough loops you can cut the final end of ribbon to match the first 7.5 cm (3'') tail or you can make one or two extra loops considerably longer than the previous loops. These can be cut in half on an angle to form tails. If you do this, to neaten the bow cut the original 7.5 cm (3'') end so that the centre loop hides it.

To secure the bow, wire through the centre loop which encased your thumb in the beginning. Make sure that all the loops have crossed properly at the back of the bow so that all the centres are caught in the wire. Twist, and bring the wire ends down together.

Alternatively, if you are tying this bow to the bottom of a sheaf or posy, tear a long strip of ribbon and pass it through the bow as if it were wire. To secure, tie ribbon firmly at the centre and bring loose ends down ready to tie around the base of the sheaf or posy.

2 DESIGN GUIDELINES

Elements of design

Like any other art form, flower arranging should be a spontaneous form of self-expression. Work from your inner feelings and inspirations. This said, it is also necessary to put those inspirations into some sort of order to produce a harmonious creation. Points to consider are:

Setting   Have you chosen the right style or design for the setting?

Balance   Does the arrangement look as if it is standing well on its own? Do you have an even distribution of flowers and foliages? Are the colours in your arrangement balanced? Is the size of the arrangement in proportion to the size of your container?

Rhythm   Does the arrangement encourage your eye to move all over it? That is, does the arrangement flow or is it stiff?

Texture   Is there variation in the surface texture of plant materials used? For example, broad flat leaves set off by dainty spiky fern, softly rounded flower heads contrasted with spiky ones?

Colour   Do the colours of the flowers clash or do they highlight each other?

Line   Is there any overcrowding of the flowers or do they all have their own space? Is the shape of the arrangement clearly defined?

Three dimensions   Make sure that your flowers are on different levels. In traditional styles different flowers should be pushed in further than others. In the layered look there are variations in the heights of different flower groupings. With a true three-dimensional effect your eye should be taken round to the sides of your work. Or does your arrangement have a 'flat' face?

General guidelines

- First ask yourself: how many flowers are available for use? What atmosphere is to be created? Where is the arrangement going to stand? Will it be standing in the centre of the table, by a wall or on a bench? All these questions will help determine the style you choose.
- When setting up bowls or containers, make sure that patterned ones are facing the correct way before you start.
- To achieve greater depth in upright arrangements when using Oasis foam, where possible have the short side of the foam towards you. Never have the foam off-centre, or corner-on—this only causes confusion when you are inserting the stems.
- For a visually pleasing effect, whether making a traditional or modern arrangement, all plant stems must appear to come from a central point.
- When pushing stems into Oasis or other base material, push from the bottom of the stem to avoid snapping it.
- Whether making a traditional or modern flower arrangement, do not fight the curve of a stem—go with it. Where you have one straight stem and one curving, use the straight one in an upright position and place the curving one to the right or left of it, depending on the curve, or at the base of the arrangement so it flows down over the edge of the container.

- Until you become experienced, gauge the required length of each stem by holding it in position against the arrangement.
- An arrangement should be in proportion to the size of the container. An upright arrangement is usually 1 ½ times the height of the container. The width of the arrangement normally does not exceed the height. In the layered look, the tallest layer of flowers may be twice the height of the container.
- Always have the smallest flowers at the outside of the arrangement, directing your eye towards the larger feature flower in the centre. This applies to top to centre and base to centre as well as to sides to centre.
- The focal or feature point in your arrangement is the centre of interest, where the viewer's eye is immediately drawn. This consists usually of the largest, loveliest flower but it can also consist of a cluster of flowers.
- When placing flowers down a line, angle them further forward or out the lower they are down the line, as in the diagram. This helps keep your arrangement well balanced and in proportion, as well as aiding a three-dimensional feel. In the layered look, stagger each layer evenly down towards the base of the container.
- As you are making it, it is a good idea to turn the arrangement around a number of times so you can view it from all angles.

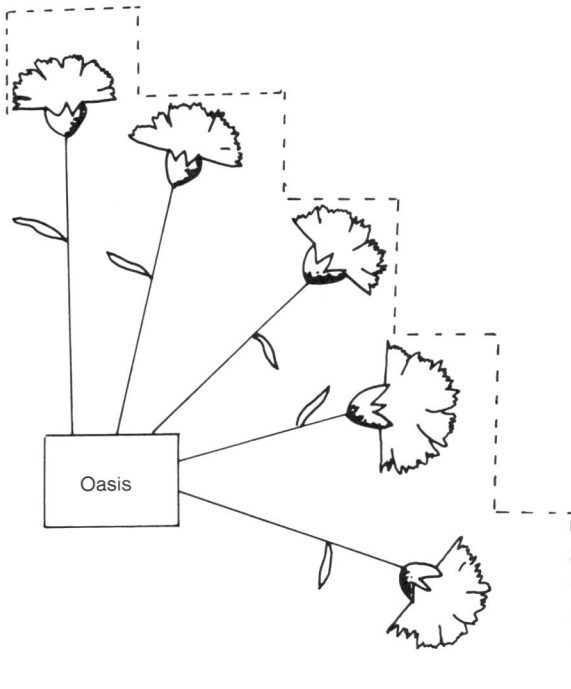

Side view of focal line

- No matter what shaped arrangement you are making, in most instances all the flowers in it will follow that shape. That is, if you make a triangle, each new set of flowers will repeat that shape within itself. Be conscious of this, and take care that you don't allow your work to become stiff.
- Do not overcrowd the flowers. Whether designing a traditional or modern style, each flower in the arrangement should have its own space and should not touch other flowers. The only time this does not apply is in the layered look, where flower heads sit side by side and often touch.
- Do not be tempted to use an extra flower just because it is left over. Know when to stop. Overcrowding flowers or foliages looks unprofessional.
- Remember to turn some of the flower heads in slightly different directions to add interest and to take your eye around the arrangement.
- Finally be sure that all the florist's foam is hidden from sight.

Glossary of terms

Feature flower   Also called 'focal flower'. The main flower or flowers in an arrangement.
Secondary flower   The second most important flower or flowers in an arrangement.
Filler flowers   Flowers used to fill in between other flowers and foliages.
Outline material   Used for making the outline of an arrangement.
Base material   Material into which plant stems are inserted—may be Oasis foam, potter's clay.
Oasis pinholder   A small round plastic disc bearing four plastic prongs onto which the base material is pushed.
Oasis Fix   A green tacky glue which comes on a roll. It is pushed onto the base of the Oasis pinholder to hold it in place.
Clay   Brown potter's clay available from craft suppliers, potters' suppliers and some flower markets.
Wire   Florist's wire. The most commonly used weights in this book are 71 mm gauge for medium weight work and 46 mm gauge for supporting delicate flowers.
Parafilm   Stretchable florist's tape. Most commonly used colour is green, but it also comes in other colours, white and brown.

3 INFORMAL ARRANGEMENTS

Driftwood No. 1

Illustrated on page 25

Note All bunches referred to throughout the book are wholesale size

Materials
upright piece of driftwood approximately 38 cm (15'') tall and approximately 8 cm (3'') in diameter
handful of potter's clay
2 lengths of 0.71 gauge wire
Oasis plastic pinholder complete with Oasis Fix
1 *Banksia hookeriana*
1 *Banksia baxterii*
2 lotus pods
1 gumnut
3 pieces tortured willow
one-third bunch velvet rush
one-quarter bunch fine tea-tree
4 stems bookleaf
one-third bunch ixodia (South Australian daisy)

Technique

Fixing base materials Using Oasis Fix, press an Oasis pinholder to the front of the trunk, about 6–8 cm (2½''–3'') down from the top. Push a handful of potter's clay onto the pinholder and press firmly against the trunk. Add extra security by bringing the two pieces of wire around from the back of the trunk and crossing them over the centre of the clay at the front. Pull wire ends firmly, using pliers, and twist tightly to secure. Don't worry if the wire digs into the clay. Cut away excess wire and fold the ends backwards into the clay. Smooth the clay down by hand. If you can't obtain potter's clay you could try using a small block of grey Oasis pushed onto the pinholder and wired in place. Clay is definitely preferable.

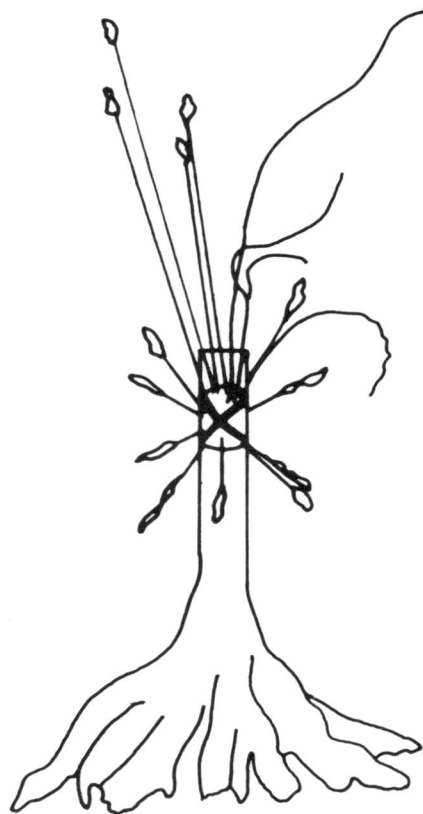

Outline Cut four long stems of velvet rush, each a slightly different length. When in place the length of the velvet rush should look in balance with the height of the driftwood, approximately equal. Starting with the longest stem insert the four pieces towards the back of the clay, at an angle, as in the first diagram. Now cut eight shorter lengths of velvet rush and insert into the sides and bottom front of the clay, as in the first diagram. Looking from the tip of the tallest piece of rush down to the shorter pieces you should be able to discern a gentle curve. Now add the tortured willow. These stems will go in front of the tallest rush stems but to the right of them.

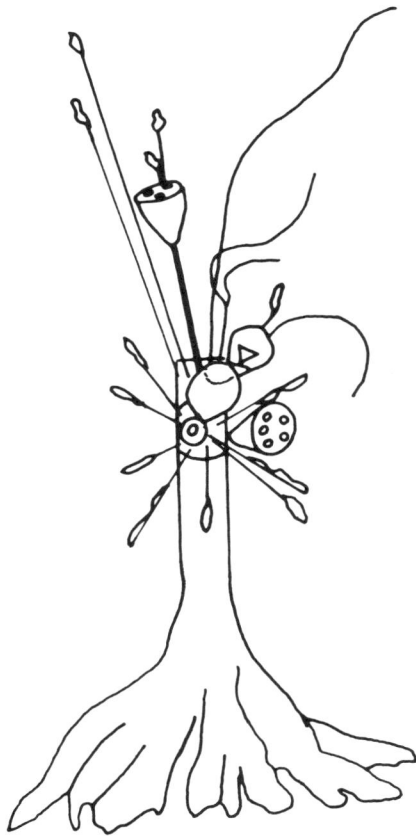

Filler flowers   It's now time to fill in all the gaps between and behind the inserted major flowers. Keep in mind texture. That's where the use of fine tea-tree is contrasted by the use of the broad leaves of bookleaf. Keep the filler flowers about 1–2 cm (½''–¾'') shorter than the shortest stems of the outline material. This helps give a three-dimensional look to the work. Use more velvet rush as filler material too. Alternate your use of filler material evenly throughout the arrangement so that you have no 'blobs' of any one type. To enhance the three-dimensional look, angle some of the side stems of filler material backwards. Push the South Australian daisy in further towards the clay than the tea-tree. Using all of the filler materials, fill in all over the arrangement so the clay is completely hidden, as in the third diagram.

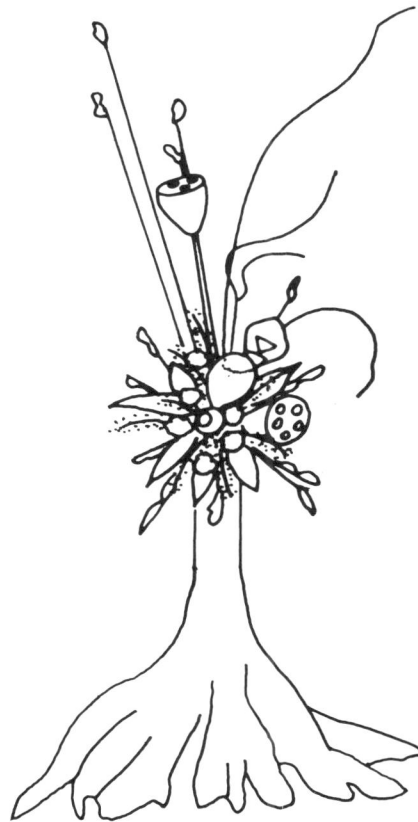

Feature flowers   Cut the first lotus pod to measure 30 cm (12'') in length. Insert it in line with but to the left of the tallest tortured willow stem. Cut the *Banksia baxterii* 10 cm (4'') below the head. Insert it in front of but to the right of the lotus pod stem. Cut the *Banksia hookeriana* stem to measure 2.5 cm (1'') below the head. Insert it in front of but to the left of the first banksia stem. This will be in the middle front of the clay. Cut the second lotus pod stem to measure 2.5 cm (1'') below the head. Insert it in front of but to the right of the *Banksia hookeriana*. This lotus pod will be in line with the first lotus pod. Now insert the gumnut just in front of and to the left of the *Banksia hookeriana*. See the second diagram.

Driftwood No. 2

Illustrated on page 25

Materials

horizontal piece of driftwood 36 cm (14'') long
    by 14 cm (5½'') wide
handful potter's clay
Oasis plastic pinholder complete with Oasis Fix
3 lengths 0.71 florist's wire
2 *Banksia hookeriana*
4 teasels
5 stems of bookleaf
half bunch coral fern
one-third bunch ruscus
one quarter bunch ixodia (South Australian daisy)

Technique

Fixing base materials   Choose a nice flat section on the face of the driftwood on which to mount the clay. Drill four holes into this section, one at each corner of an imaginary square, right through the wood. Push the end of one wire through a hole and push the other end through the diagonally opposite hole. Fix the Oasis pinholder to the centre of the 'square' using Oasis Fix and push a lump of clay onto it. Bring the wire ends across the clay diagonally and twist together using pliers. Cut off the excess wire, bend the twisted wire ends back in towards the clay and smooth over any unevenness in the clay with your hand.

In this case the driftwood had grooves in one end into which I squashed another small amount of clay for a miniature flower arrangement

duplicating the main arrangement, and wired it into place using the third strand of wire fastened over the centre of the clay.

Outline   Cut one long piece of coral fern measuring 32 cm (12½''). Place it in the centre back of the clay, angling the stem straight up and down. Leave enough clay behind the coral fern to place the foliage in later. Cut two pieces of coral fern about 16 cm (6'') long and insert into the clay in line with the first piece, one to the left and one to the right of it. Cut four pieces of fern 10 cm (4'') long and space out as in the first diagram, one in the centre of each side of the clay and one lower down each side but not at the bottom; use two pieces each 6 cm (2¼'') long at the bottom, as in the first diagram. All stems should be angled towards the centre like spokes in a wheel. When you look at the tips of each piece of outline material you should be able to make out the shape of a softly rounded triangle. Now move down to the small mound of clay at the end of the driftwood piece. Insert one longer piece of coral fern in the centre back and four shorter pieces around the perimeter of the clay as in the diagram.

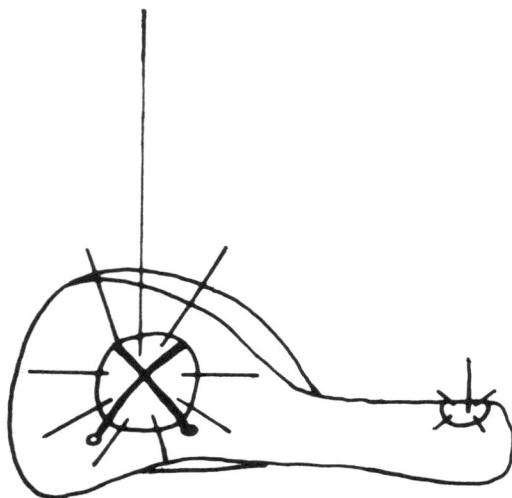

Foliage   Following the second diagram, and using the ruscus, cut one stem 24 cm (9½'') long to stand behind the first piece of coral fern. Push into the clay, sloping it *slightly* backwards. Then

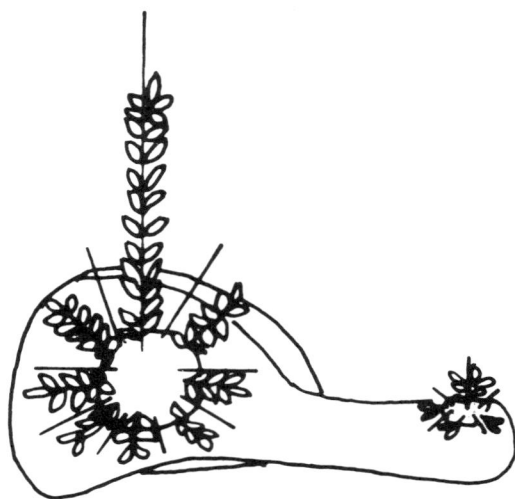

cut seven pieces of ruscus 10 cm (4'') long and push into the clay between the coral fern stems. Repeat this sequence, using a lesser number of stems, in the small arrangement at the end of the driftwood.

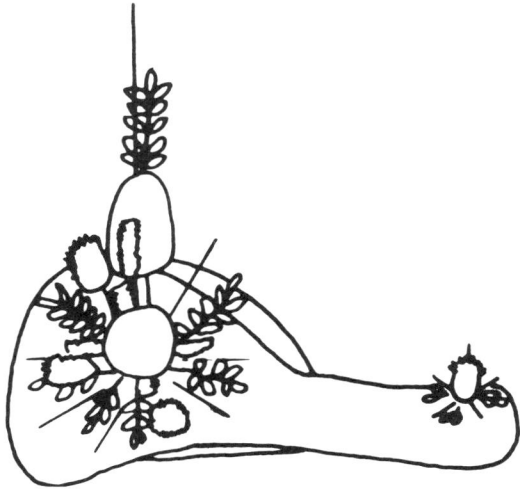

Feature flowers   It's time to place the *Banksia hookeriana* heads, following the third diagram. To keep a balanced look these heavy flowers should be placed low down towards the centre of the arrangement. The larger of the two banksias will go in the centre of the clay, facing outwards, while the other will be positioned above it, in front of the tallest piece of outline material. I always suggest holding the two in position against the clay to gauge their correct heights before actually cutting and placing them. When you are convinced the balance looks correct, insert the taller, smaller banksia first, in front of the tallest piece of outline material. Then insert the second banksia in front of the first, but lower down. There should be approximately 10 cm (4'') between the top of the first banksia and the top of the second.

Now insert the four teasels into the clay. The first will be in line with the first banksia but to its left. Note the angle in the third diagram. Place the other two teasels into the clay in the main arrangement in the positions indicated, then insert the fourth in an upright position, low down in the clay, in the small arrangement at the end of the driftwood.

Filler flowers   Fill in the arrangement using short pieces of coral fern and a few stems of bookleaf. These leaves should not dominate the arrangement but should be placed low down amongst the flowers for texture. See the fourth diagram. A few short stems of ruscus can also be used. Dot stems of South Australian daisy evenly throughout the arrangement. These should be shorter than the coral fern and ruscus stems by about 1 cm (¼''–½''). Don't forget to fill in between the flowers in the small arrangement too. In both cases all the clay should be covered. Remember also to angle some side stems a little toward the back of the arrangement for a three-dimensional effect.

Modern bowl No. 1

Illustrated on page 26

Materials

flat round bowl approximately 23 cm (9'')
   diameter
Oasis plastic pinholder complete with Oasis Fix
block of Oasis foam approximately 10 × 8 cm
   (4'' × 3'')
   OR a lump of potter's clay the size of a small
   tennis ball
2 grasstree spears
2 *Banksia prionotes*
5 large everlasting daisies
9 teasels
1 bunch spinning gum
one-third bunch basket flower

Technique

Fixing base materials Press Oasis Fix to bottom
of pinholder and press pinholder down into centre
bottom of bowl. Push Oasis (or clay) firmly onto
pinholder. The long side of the Oasis should be
facing you.

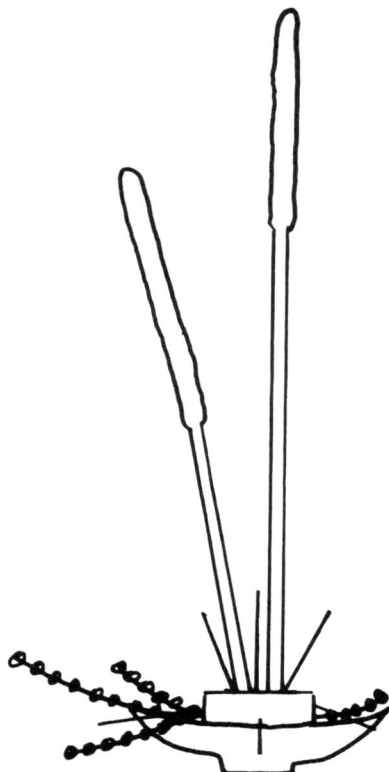

Outline Cut one grasstree spear to measure
75 cm (30'') and the second to measure 56 cm
(22''). Insert the longer one to the right of the
centre back of the Oasis. Position the second spear
to the left of the centre back of the Oasis, in line
with the first spear, as in the first diagram.

Now cut six pieces of spinning gum (represented by the straight lines in the first diagram).
Cut the three upright pieces to measure
approximately 15 cm (6''). The two side pieces
will also measure 15 cm (6'') while the front stem
should be about 10 cm (4'') long. Place the
upright stems of spinning gum in a line behind
the grasstree spears, the one in the centre back
of the Oasis upright, the other two angled in
towards the centre. Insert the side stems of
spinning gum in the centre sides of the Oasis,
angling them down over the edge of the bowl.
Insert the front piece in the centre front of the
Oasis, again angling it down over the bowl.

Now cut four pieces of basket flower. The
longest piece should be about 21 cm (8''), two
about 17 cm (7'') and the fourth about 12 cm
(5''). Insert the first three stems into the left-hand
side of the Oasis, with the longest piece in the
centre of the side. All stems will angle slightly up
towards the ceiling, as shown in the first diagram.
Insert the shortest piece of basket flower into the
centre of the right-hand side of the Oasis, angling
it slightly upwards. This completes the outline.

Feature flowers The larger banksia will be cut with
a shorter stem, and will be the main feature
flower. Cut the smaller banksia to measure 12 cm
(5'') under the head and the larger one to measure
9 cm (3½''). Insert the smaller banksia into the
top of the Oasis in front of the longest grasstree
stem. Insert the short stem of the larger banksia
into the top of the Oasis in front of the first
banksia, angling the head forward so that it is
facing you. See the second diagram.

Secondary flowers Cut the stems of the nine teasels
to measure 8 cm (3'') below the head. Insert into
the right-hand side and right-hand top of the
Oasis, following the shape shown in the third
diagram. The inside teasels are pushed further
into the Oasis, so that they are shorter than the
teasels on the outer edge of the arrangement.
(Note that not all the teasels are indicated on the

Filling in Now cover the visible Oasis by filling in. The left-hand side of the arrangement is filled in using short pieces of spinning gum. Go all over the Oasis on that section of the arrangement, remembering that the gum should not hide the everlasting daisies from view. Fill in the right-hand side of the arrangement, using a few pieces of spinning gum but mostly using short pieces of basket flower. Fill in the front and back of the arrangement using short pieces of spinning gum.

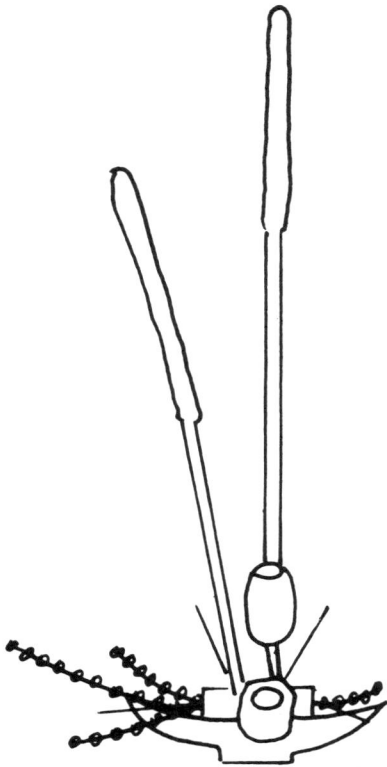

diagram.) Now, using the five everlasting daisies, cut the stems to measure about 12.5 cm (5'') from top to bottom. Follow the shape shown in the photograph on page 26, leaving one daisy stem extending beyond the others on the left-hand side of the arrangement. Insert stems into left-hand side and left-hand top of Oasis.

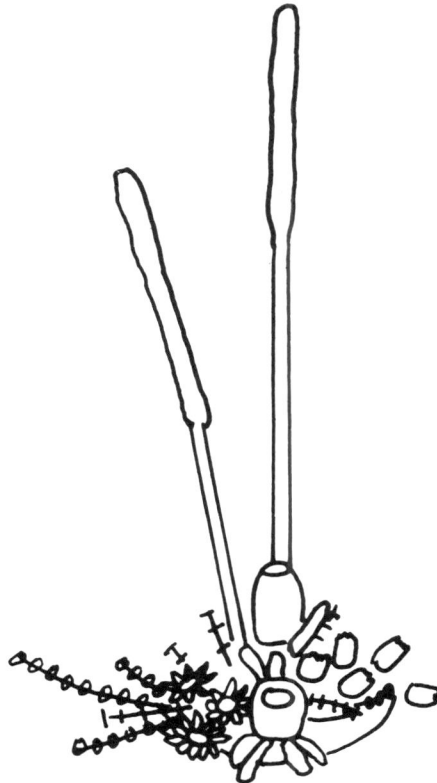

Modern Bowl No. 2

Illustrated on page 26

Materials

flat round bowl approximately 23 cm (9'')
  diameter
Oasis plastic pinholder complete with Oasis Fix
block of Oasis approximately 10 cm × 8 cm ×
  5 cm (4'' × 3'' × 2'')
  OR a lump of potter's clay the size of a small
  tennis ball
one-quarter bunch basket flower
5 pieces smoke bush
2 *Banksia prionotes*
3 *Banksia baxterii*
half bunch ixodia (South Australian daisy)
11 large everlasting daisies
half bunch spinning gum
small cluster of large gumnuts (about 5)

Technique

Fixing base materials Press Oasis Fix to bottom
of pinholder and press down into centre bottom
of bowl. Push Oasis (or clay) firmly onto
pinholder. Position the Oasis with the longest side
facing you (to the front).

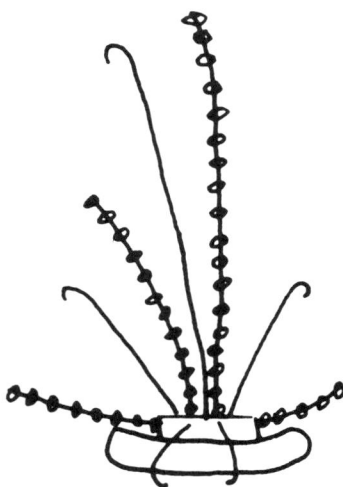

Outline Cut four pieces of basket flower, the
longest stem 49 cm (19''), then one piece 34 cm
(13'') and two pieces 17 cm (7'') long. Insert the
longest stem of basket flower in an upright
position in the centre back of the Oasis, on an
imaginary line 2 cm (¾'') in from the back of

the Oasis. Insert the second longest piece of basket
flower in an upright position to the left of and
in line with the first piece. Insert the two short
pieces of basket flower, one into the centre of the
left-hand side of the Oasis, one into the centre
of the right-hand side. Keep any curve in the side
foliage facing upwards.

Cut five pieces of smoke bush. The longest will
measure about 47 cm (18½''), two pieces will
measure 32 cm (12½'') and the last two will each
measure 11 cm (4½''). Insert the longest piece
of smoke bush in an upright position between and
in line with the first two pieces of basket flower.
Insert the next two longest pieces in line with the
upright basket flower and angled towards the
centre, one to the left of the second piece of basket
flower and one to the right of the first piece of
basket flower. Insert the two short pieces of smoke
bush into the front of the Oasis, one to the left
of the centre point and one to the right of it,
angling them down over the edge of the bowl as
in the first diagram.

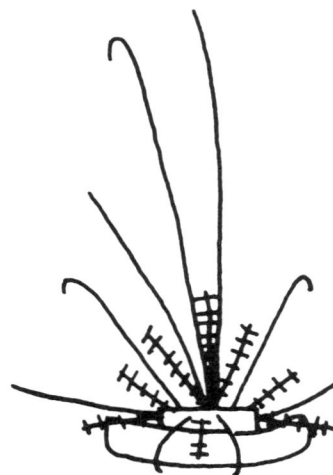

Foliage Cut a piece of spinning gum 20 cm (8'')
long. Insert it into the centre back of the Oasis
behind the basket flower. Cut two pieces of
spinning gum measuring 18 cm (7''). Insert one
piece in line with and to the left of the first piece
of gum and the other in line with and to the right
of the first piece of gum. Both pieces are angled
towards the centre of the Oasis. Cut two pieces

20

of spinning gum each measuring 16 cm (6''). Insert one to the left of the gum just inserted and one to the right of the right-hand gum just inserted. All these pieces of gum will be angled slightly backwards—see the second diagram. Now cut two pieces of gum measuring 13 cm (5'') each. Insert one into the left-hand side of the Oasis just above the basket flower stem and one likewise into the right-hand side of the Oasis. Angle the stems to hang down over the edge of the container.

Cut another piece of gum measuring 11 cm (4½'') in length. Insert this into the centre front of the Oasis between the two pieces of smoke bush. Check the second diagram again.

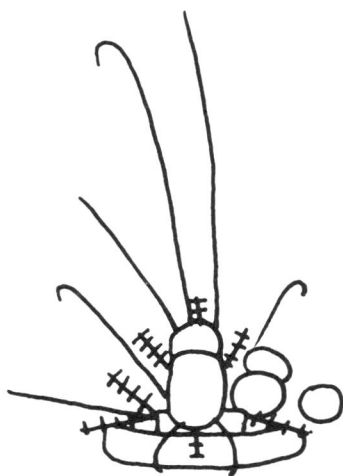

Feature flowers   Choose the larger *Banksia prionotes* head to be the main feature flower. Cut its stem to measure 6 cm (2½'') in length under the flower head. Cut the stem of the smaller banksia to measure 10 cm (4'') under the flower head. Insert the taller banksia into the top of the Oasis, just left of the centre and in front of the basket flower and smoke bush, with the head facing upwards. Insert the other banksia in front of the first one, as near as possible to the front edge of the Oasis, as in the third diagram. Now take the *Banksia baxterii* heads, cutting one to measure

12 cm (5'') below the flower head and the other two to measure 6 cm (2½'') below the flower head. The longest stem is inserted horizontally into the Oasis, close to the centre of the right side, so it sits parallel to the table. Insert one of the remaining banksias in the right-hand top of the Oasis with its head angled slightly towards the back of the arrangement, and the other one in the front right-hand top side of the Oasis with its head angled at 45° to the first *Banksia baxterii*. See the photograph on page 26.

Secondary flowers   Cut the South Australian daisy stems to measure approximately 9 cm (3½''). Insert these into the right-hand top and right-hand side of the Oasis next to the *Banksia prionotes*. Angle the stems in toward the centre of the Oasis.

Now take the bunch of gumnuts, cutting the stem to measure 5 cm (2'') below the nuts. Push these into the top of the Oasis immediately to the right of the *Banksia prionotes*. Cut the stems of the everlasting daisies so they measure 9 cm (3½'') from top to bottom. Dot these evenly over the right-hand top front and sides of the Oasis. Remember to angle the stems towards the centre.

Filling in   Use very short pieces of spinning gum and basket flower to fill in all the gaps displaying Oasis. Don't let any of this filling in cover the banksias or everlasting daisies from sight.

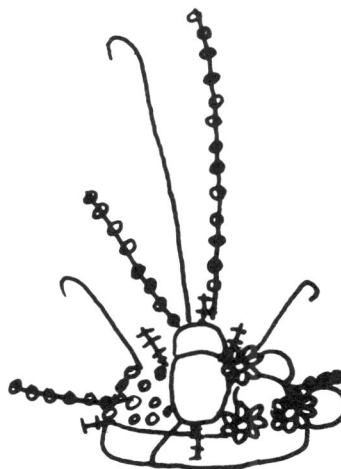

4 FORMAL ARRANGEMENTS

Topiary tree

Illustrated on page 27

Materials

glazed or terracotta pot approximately 9 cm
    (3½'') diameter and 7 cm (2¾'') tall
enough plaster of Paris to fill pot
heaped tablespoon potter's clay
plastic Oasis pinholder complete with Oasis Fix
enough coconut fibre to decorate top of pot
stick about 28 cm (11'') long and 1 cm (½'')
    diameter
ball of grey Oasis the size of a small tennis ball
craft glue
one-quarter bunch fine tea-tree
one-quarter bunch cauliflower morrison
half bunch fairy sago or gypsophila (baby's breath)
10 large everlasting daisies
11 small clusters of mount-wired Mexican daisies

Technique

Fixing base materials Press Oasis pinholder
complete with Oasis Fix onto centre bottom of
pot. Push clay onto pinholder. Now push the top
of the stick into the Oasis ball for about 4 cm
(1½''), then withdraw it. Add glue inside the hole
in the Oasis ball and to the end of the stick. Push
the ball back onto stick.

Now push the lower end of the stick into the
clay in an upright position. Mix plaster of Paris
into a sloppy paste with water and pour it into
pot. Fill the pot nearly up to the rim, leaving
enough space to add the coconut fibre later on.
Set aside until plaster of Paris has set and the
Oasis ball is firmly glued. You may have to wait
overnight depending on the glue.

Outline Cut tea-tree to measure 10 cm (4'') in
length and insert evenly all over the Oasis ball.
The ball should look like a sputnik when you've
finished, as in the first diagram.

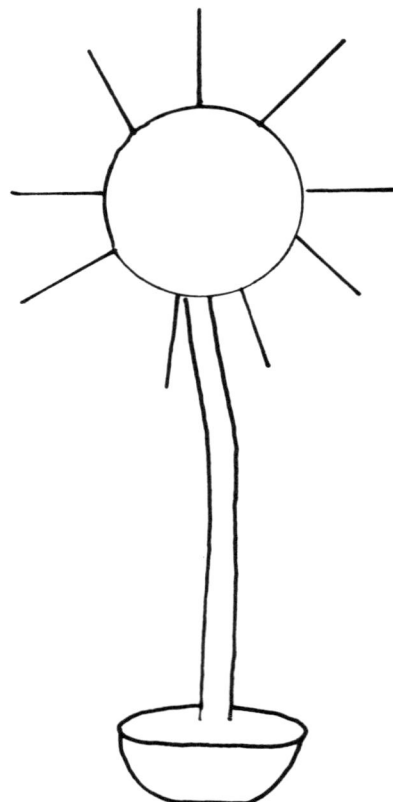

Feature flowers   Cut the everlasting daisy a little shorter than the tea-tree and insert evenly between the tea-tree, as shown in the second diagram.

Filler flowers   Insert the cauliflower morrison close to the surface of the ball, with the stems cut shorter than the daisies. Space evenly all over the ball. Insert the small clusters of mount-wired Mexican daisies so that the heads are on the same level as the tea-tree. Do the same with the fairy sago or gypsophila. Fill in any gaps using left-over tea-tree and cauliflower morrison. Cover the surface of the plaster of Paris with fluffed up coconut fibre.

Layered look in a round terracotta pot

Illustrated on page 28

Materials

terracotta pot approximately 9 cm (3½'')
    diameter and 7.5 cm (3'') tall
handful of potter's clay *OR* enough mortar mix
    to fill pot
plastic Oasis pinholder complete with Oasis Fix
sufficient raffia to go around the pot and finish
    with a bow *OR* use paper ribbon
craft glue
7 everlasting daisies
one-quarter bunch wheat
one-quarter bunch ixodia (South Australian
    daisy)
one-quarter bunch German statice

Technique

Fixing base materials   If using clay, first press the Oasis pinholder complete with Oasis Fix to the bottom of the pot, covering the hole. Then push the mound of clay onto the pinholder. The clay can almost fill the pot. If using mortar, mix with water until a thick paste forms. Cover the hole in the pot with a tiny square of plastic and pour the mortar mix into the pot almost to the rim. Use before it sets.

First layer   Take the wheat and group all the heads together at the same level. Cut the stems to measure 28 cm (11''). Holding the stems near the bottom, push them vertically into the centre of the base material, as in the first diagram.

Second layer   There are no hard rules for spacings between layers. Basically your guide will be visual balance between the levels. In this arrangement I measured down 4 cm (1½'') from the base of the ears of wheat as a guide to the height of the second layer. Take the everlasting daisies and cut their stems to measure 19 cm (7½'') from top to bottom. Insert the stems into the base material in a circle around the wheat.

Third layer   Cut the South Australian daisy stems to measure 12 cm (4¾'') from top to bottom. When inserted into the base material their heads will sit 7 cm (2¾'') below the heads of the everlasting daisies. Place them in a circle around the everlasting daisies, as in the second diagram.

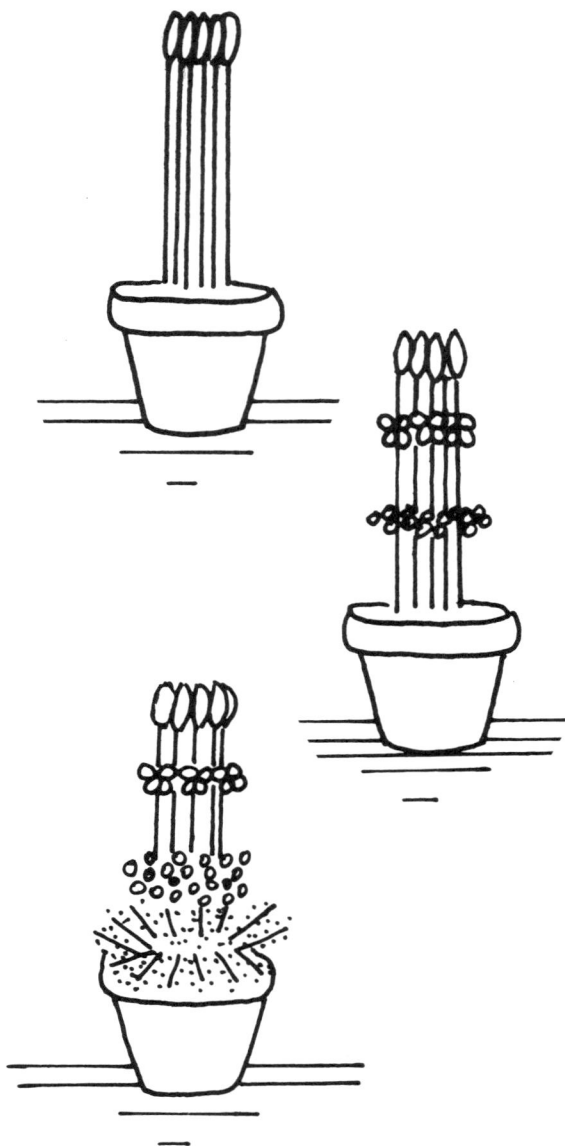

Final layer   Cut the stems of the German statice to measure 9 cm (3½''). Insert the statice to sit just underneath the South Australian daisies, sticking out over the sides of the bowl in a circle around the South Australian daisies.

Finishing   Spot a blob of glue on the back of the pot at the level you wish to place the raffia. Wind the raffia (or paper ribbon) around the pot and tie into a bow at the front. Spot some glue behind the bow to hold it in place.

Driftwood No. 1, an informal arrangement
(page 14)

Driftwood No. 2, an informal arrangement
(page 16)

Modern bowl No. 1, an informal arrangement
(page 18)

Modern bowl No. 2, an informal arrangement
(page 20)

This formal Topiary Tree is described on page 22

A formal layered look in a rectangular basket (opposite)

A formal layered look in a round terracotta pot (page 24)

28

Layered look in a rectangular basket

Illustrated on opposite page

Materials

rectangular basket 13 cm wide × 13 cm deep
   × 23 cm long (5'' × 5'' × 9'')
plastic Oasis pinholder complete with Oasis Fix
standard size block of Oasis foam
17 stems wheat
17 stems larkspur
small bunch lavender
7 roses
half bunch ixodia (South Australian daisy)
one-quarter bunch nigella
handful sphagnum moss

Technique

Fixing base materials   Cut Oasis foam to fit basket.
Press Oasis pinholder to base of basket and push
foam onto it.

First layer   Cut the wheat to measure 45 cm
(18''). Insert vertically in a horizontal line across
the back of the Oasis as in the first diagram.

Second layer   Following the second diagram, cut
the larkspur so that the tops, when in place, sit
just below the level of the wheat heads. Insert
vertically in a horizontal line in front of the wheat.

Third layer   Cut the lavender stems so their tops
sit about 8 cm (3'') below the top of the larkspur
when in place. Insert vertically in a horizontal
line in front of the larkspur.

Fourth layer   Cut the rose stems so they sit about
6 cm (2½'') down from the top of the lavender
when in place. Insert vertically in a horizontal
line in front of the lavender.

Fifth layer   Cut the South Australian daisy stems
so they sit just below the rose heads when in place.
Insert vertically in a horizontal line in front of
the roses.

Seventh layer   Cut the nigella so some stems are
tall enough to sit under the heads of the South
Australian daisies and others so they sit just above
the edge of the container. Cluster together in a
horizontal line along the Oasis in front of the

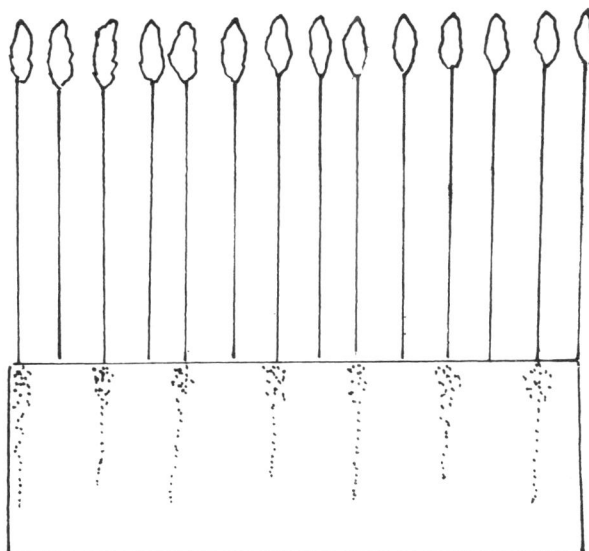

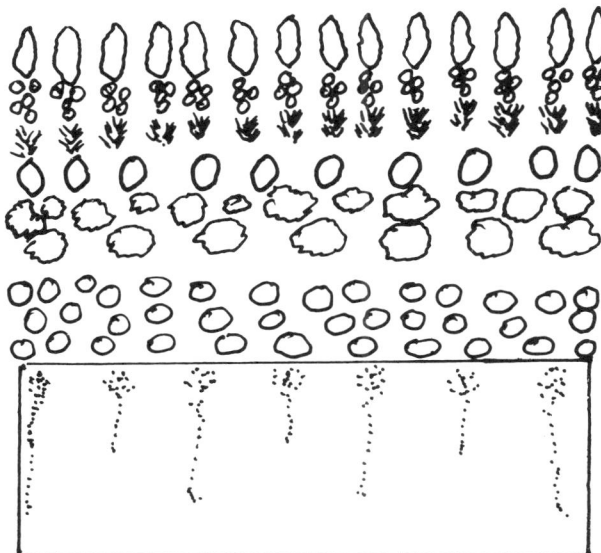

South Australian daisies. Study the photograph
on the opposite page to appreciate the effect
required.

Finishing   Spread the sphagnum moss over any
exposed Oasis and around the stems of the flowers
in the top of the container.

29

5 GIFT IDEAS

Topiary tree on a wooden board

Illustrated on page 45

Materials

wooden breadboard 33 cm × 24 cm (13″ × 9½″)
8 cm (3″) diameter half terracotta pot and
    matching half saucer
half grey Oasis foam ball, smaller than a tennis
    ball
quarter block green Oasis foam
small tortured willow twig approximately 14 cm
    (5½″) long and 3 mm (¼″) thick
handful sphagnum moss
hot glue gun and stick of heavy duty yellow glue
27 pussytails
one-quarter bunch cauliflower morrison
one-quarter bunch German statice
3 bushy stems tea-tree
3 bushy stems fern rush
tiny ceramic frog
3 tiny ceramic mushrooms
2 tiny brass screw eyes
length of 0.71 gauge florist's wire

Technique

Fixing base materials Take the quarter block of
Oasis. Lay it down flat and place the half
terracotta pot on top of it. Push the pot down hard
onto the Oasis so that its interior becomes filled
with Oasis. Cut around the shape of the pot with
a knife. Cut the back of the Oasis flush with the
pot and remove the excess foam.

Now rub the terracotta pot and saucer with a
cloth to remove all dust. Using the glue gun, glue
the raw edge of the saucer. Measuring 2 cm (¾″)
up from the bottom of the board, centre the
saucer at the base of the board and push down
firmly to glue it to the board. Glue the edges of
the terracotta pot and all over the back of the
Oasis. Centre on board inside the saucer and push

firmly into place. Allow time for the glue to dry,
preferably overnight.

Take the tortured willow twig and push the tip
into the centre of the Oasis foam half ball.
Withdraw. Push the other end of the twig down
into the centre back of the Oasis inside the pot.
Glue the back of the Oasis ball and the hole made
by the twig. Centre the Oasis ball approximately
4 cm (1½″) down from the top edge of the board,
inserting the top of the twig into the hole at the
same time. Press down on the ball firmly. See
the first diagram.

Moss Glue a band of moss along the bottom
edge of the board across its width. Glue moss on
top of the Oasis in the terracotta pot, allowing
some to hang over the edges. Glue the frog into

30

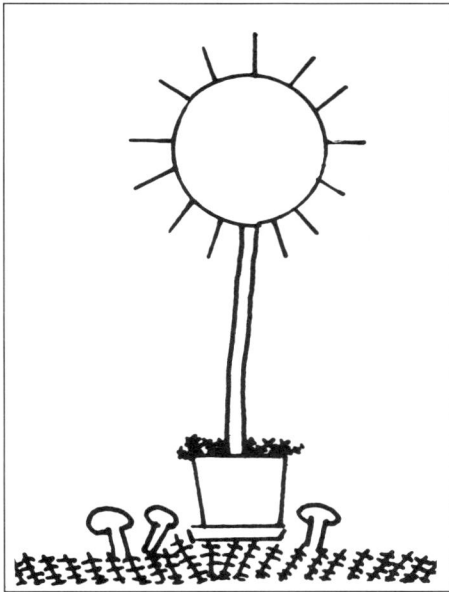

statice. Push clumps in all over the ball. Make sure the edges of the ball are well covered so you can't see it from the sides of the board. Now take three pussytails at a time and insert these clusters evenly all over the ball until all the pussytails have been used. The pussytails can stand out from the ball at about the same height as the tea-tree and German statice. Finish filling in by adding the fern rush evenly throughout the arrangement. There should be no Oasis visible to the eye.

Finishing off At the back of the board measure down 10 cm (4'') from the top edge and about 3 cm (1¼'') on either side. Screw in the brass eye screws at these points. String the length of 0.71 gauge wire between the screws.

place on top of the moss in the pot. Glue the mushrooms into place at the bottom of the pot, on either side of the saucer, as in the second diagram.

Outline Take the tea-tree and break into pieces no more than 4 cm (1½'') long. Insert all over the Oasis ball, following the shape of the ball. The flowers should not go beyod the top edge of the board. With the German statice go all over the ball in the same manner, following the second diagram.

Filler flowers Fill in between the stems of tea-tree and German statice using pieces of cauliflower morrison shorter than the tea-tree and German

Fridge magnet

Illustrated on page 45

Materials

1 m florist's paper ribbon
fridge magnet
hot glue gun and regular white glue stick
1 everlasting daisy
4 ears of wheat
2 sprigs eucalypt leaves
2 stems German statice
40 Mexican daisies
3 lengths 0.71 gauge florist's wire

Technique

Fixing base materials   Using the paper ribbon make a flat 4-looped bow wired in the centre (page 9). The outside loops should be 9 cm (3½'') long and the two final loops 6 cm (2½'') long. Make the tails 5 cm (2'') long.

Outline   Cut the wheat ears to each measure 34 cm (13½'') from tip of head to end of the stalk. Using the glue gun, glue wheat to bow, leaving heads close to bow centre and stalks trailing downwards, as in the first diagram.

Foliage   Cut the eucalypt sprigs to measure 5 cm (2'') including stalk. Glue one sprig to the left and one to the right of the wheat, on top of it.

Filler flowers   Make four clusters of flowers 7 cm (2¾'') long, using German statice for the background and Mexican daisies for the foreground. Mount-wire using 0.71 gauge wire. Glue the clustered flowers in a circle on top of the eucalypt leaves, following the photo on page 45.

Feature flower   Cut the head of the paper daisy from its wire stem if it has one. Glue the flower-head into the centre of the circle of clustered flowers.

Finishing off   Glue magnet to the back of the paper bow.

Door hanger

Illustrated on page 45

Materials

diecut wooden door hanger
hot glue gun and yellow heavy duty stick of glue
7 cm (2¾'') diameter half terracotta pot
one-quarter block green Oasis foam
4.5 cm (1¾'') strip of metallic ribbon 1.5 cm (¾'') wide
20 cm (8'') florist's paper ribbon 1.5 cm (¾'') wide
5 ears of wheat
2 stems fern rush
30 Mexican daisies

Technique

Fixing base materials   Take the quarter block of Oasis. Lay it down flat and place the half pot on top of it. Push the pot down hard onto the Oasis so that its interior becomes filled with Oasis. Cut around the shape of the pot with a knife, removing the excess Oasis. Cut the back of the Oasis flush with the pot. Rub the pot with a cloth to remove all dust. Using the glue gun, glue the edges of the terracotta pot and all over the back of the foam. Centre the pot at the base of the door hanger. Cut the metallic ribbon to measure and glue it around the rim of the pot. Leave to dry, preferably overnight.

Outline   Insert the five ears of wheat into the back of the Oasis in a straight line from one side of the pot to the other. Keep the wheat below the round door-handle opening, following the first diagram.

Filler flowers   Insert the fern rush into the Oasis in front of the wheat and just below it. Cut 20 Mexican daisy stems short enough to fit below the fern rush and centre in the pot in front of the fern rush, as shown in the second diagram.

Finishing off   Using the paper ribbon make a small fancy flower bow (see page 10). Centre this at the top of the door hanger and glue into place. Take the remaining Mexican daisies and cut the stems fairly short. Combine with a little fern rush and glue into the centre of the bow, under the middle loop.

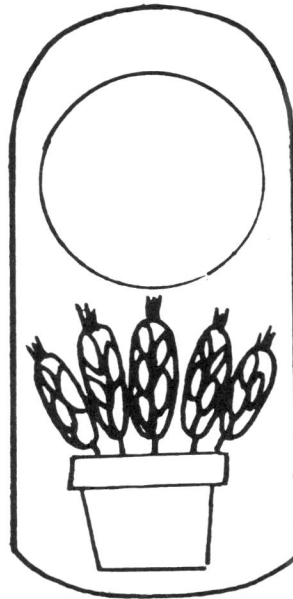

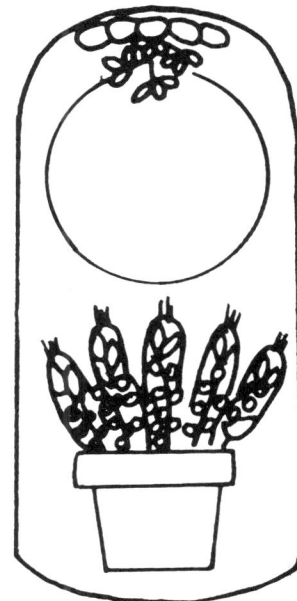

33

Terracotta pot picture

Illustrated on page 45

Materials
wooden picture frame 31 cm (12½'') square
7 cm (2¾'') diameter half terracotta pot complete
   with half saucer
hot glue gun and yellow heavy duty stick of glue
one-quarter block green Oasis foam
1 m (39'') raffia ribbon
10 stems lavender
4 small rosebuds
4 pieces banksia leaf
small clump baeckea flower
handful sphagnum moss

Technique

Fixing base materials   Take the quarter block of
Oasis. Lay it down flat and place the half pot on
top of it. Push the pot down hard onto the Oasis
so that its interior becomes filled with Oasis. Cut
around the shape of the pot with a knife,
removing the excess Oasis. Cut the back of the
Oasis flush with the pot. Now rub the terracotta
pot and saucer with a cloth to remove all dust.

   Using the glue gun, glue the cut edges of the
saucer and centre it at the base of the picture
frame, within the frame. Next, glue the edges of
the terracotta pot and all over the back of the
Oasis. Centre pot inside saucer. Push down firmly
to stick in place. Leave to dry.

Outline   Cut the lavender stems to measure
18 cm (7''). Insert in the back of the Oasis so they
stand below the edge of the picture frame by 4 cm
(1½'').

Feature flowers   Cut the rose stems to measure
10 cm (4'') below the buds. Insert in Oasis in
front of the lavender stems. The buds sit about
6 cm (2½'') below the top of the lavender, as
shown in the first diagram.

Foliage   Following the second diagram, cut the
banksia leaf to measure 11 cm (4½''). Remove
excess leaves at the base of the stems where they
will be inserted into the Oasis. Insert in the Oasis
in front of the roses. The tops of the banksia leaf
will sit just below the buds.

Filler flower   Cut enough short pieces of baeckea
to fill the space in front of the banksia leaf and

insert into Oasis. The baeckea sits 4 cm (1½'')
below the top of the banksia leaf.

Finishing off   Glue sphagnum moss over
remaining visible Oasis. Trail a little down over
the right-hand side of the pot. Cut a strip of raffia
and glue across the top of the pot, under the raised
edge. Make a small raffia bow and glue in centre
of raffia strip.

Country style wreath

Illustrated on page 45

Materials

43 cm (17'') wreath base
hot glue gun and stick of regular glue
bunch 0.46 or 0.70 florist's wire
one-quarter bunch eucalypt leaves
one-half bunch fern rush
one-half bunch Chinese puzzle
8 *Dryandra formosa* heads
bunch wheat
half bunch gypsophila
half bunch ixodia (South Australian daisy)
one-third bunch nigella
one-third bunch cauliflower morrison
4 large gumnuts
1.5 m (60'') crinkly paper ribbon

Technique

Fixing base materials　Cut wire lengths into thirds. Halve the bunch of wheat and put one half aside for finishing off. Divide each bunch of flower and foliage, including the wheat, into bunches of four and mount-wire on single legs (page 8). The dryandra heads will be paired.

Making the wreath　Leave enough room at the centre top of the wreath for a large bow. To the left of this space start positioning the foliages and flowers. Following the first diagram, first glue the eucalypt leaves to the wreath base, standing them vertically. Then glue on the fern rush, angled slightly to the right, covering the stems of the eucalypt. Then glue the Chinese puzzle to the wreath base, angled slightly to the left with the stems covering the stems of the fern rush. Now glue the pairs of *Dryandra formosa* heads to the wreath with one of the heads centred over the previous stems. Glue the wheat so it's angled slightly to the left with the stems covering the dryandra stems. Glue the ixodia so it is centred on the wreath with the flower heads covering the previous stems. Glue the nigella so it is angled slightly to the left with the stems covering the ixodia stems. Then glue the cauliflower morrison angled to the right with the stems covering the nigella stems.

Now it's time to start the sequence all over again, with the eucalypt leaves centred so the leaves are covering the previous stems. Continue like this all around the wreath. You should end with another set of eucalypt leaves to the right of the gap left for the bow.

Finishing off　Glue the four gumnuts evenly around the wreath. Take the wheat which was set aside earlier. Cut the stems to measure 38 cm (15''). Tie wire around the centre of the bundle of wheat to secure it. Now glue the centre of the wheat to the centre of the gap so the wheat hangs down toward the centre point of the wreath. Make a 6-looped fancy flower bow and glue over the top of the glued wheat (see page 10).

6 LARGE ARRANGEMENTS

Banksias in a square terracotta pot *Illustrated on page 47*

Materials

terracotta pot 16 cm (6'') square and 8 cm (3'')
  deep
half block green or grey Oasis
Oasis pinholder complete with Oasis Fix
4 large *Banksia prionotes*
one-third bunch *Dryandra formosa*
one-third bunch cauliflower morrison
half bunch eucalypt leaves

Technique

Fixing base materials Make sure the terracotta
bowl's interior is dust-free, then press the Oasis
pinholder complete with Oasis fix onto the centre
base of the bowl. Trim the Oasis to the size of
the bowl and push onto the pinholder.

Foliage Cut the first stem of eucalypt to measure
38 cm (15''). Measure 1.5 cm (½'') in from the
back of the Oasis on the centre line and insert
this stem into the Oasis in an upright position.
Cut the second eucalypt stem to measure 33 cm
(13''). Insert this into the Oasis on a slight angle,
in line with the first piece and to the right of it.
Cut the third eucalypt stem 30 cm (11½'') long
and insert into the Oasis on a slight angle, in line
with the first piece but to the left of it, following
the first diagram.

Cut two pieces of eucalypt 12 cm (5'') long.
Insert one into the centre of the left-hand side of
the Oasis and one into the centre of the right-
hand side, as in the first diagram. Cut six more
lengths of eucalypt roughly 12 cm (5'') long, but
no longer than that. Insert one into the centre
front of the Oasis and one into the centre back.
Position the remaining four stems into the four

corners of the Oasis block, angled towards the
centre, as in the first diagram.

Feature flowers Cut the first banksia stem to
measure 20 cm (8'') below the head. Insert into
Oasis vertically, in front of the first eucalypt stem.
Cut the second banksia stem to measure 14 cm
(5½'') below the head. Insert at a slight angle,
only just leaning forward, in front of and to the
right of the first banksia stem. Cut the third
banksia stem to measure 12 cm (4¾'') below the
head. Insert at a slight angle, leaning a little

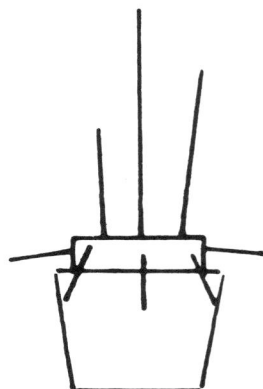

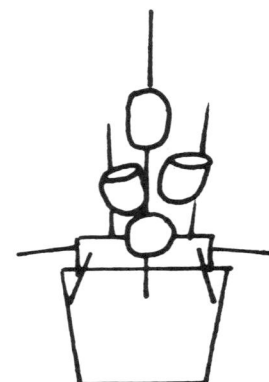

forward in front of and to the left of the second banksia stem. Cut the remaining banksia stem 6 cm (2½'') under the flower head and insert into the Oasis at a 45° angle, facing forward, in front of the third banksia and in line with the first See. the second diagram.

Secondary flowers   Dot the *Dryandra formosa* stems evenly throughout the arrangement, moving in between the banksias and out to the sides, back and front of your work. Vary stem lengths from long between the back banksias to shorter at the sides. All these stems should be shorter than the banksias and the foliage.

Filler flowers   Fill in between the banksias and dryandra, first using cauliflower morrison graduated in length like the dryandra. Fill in the remaining gaps in the arrangement using the rest of the eucalypt foliage. Make sure that no one flower or piece of foliage dominates the arrangement but that your work is an even blend.

Banksias and proteas in a tall vase *Illustrated on page 46*

Materials

pottery vase 36 cm (14'') tall × 12 cm (5'')
   diameter
bunch stirlingia bud
half bunch bookleaf
half bunch nitens morrison
half bunch ixodia (South Australian daisy)
3 *Protea neriifolia*
3 *Banksia hookeriana*

Technique

Fixing base materials Scrunch up enough newspaper to two-thirds fill the vase.

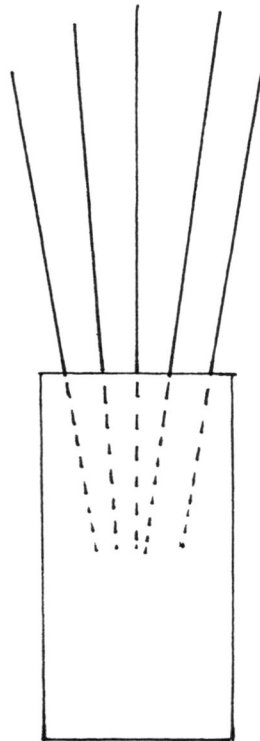

Outline Take five stems of stirlingia and insert into vase with the tallest piece in the centre back of the vase. The other pieces will graduate slightly in length. Angle stems towards centre as in the first diagram.

Foliage Insert five stems of bookleaf in front of the five stems of stirlingia, making the bookleaf approximately 10 cm (4'') shorter than the stirlingia. Again slightly graduate the lengths.

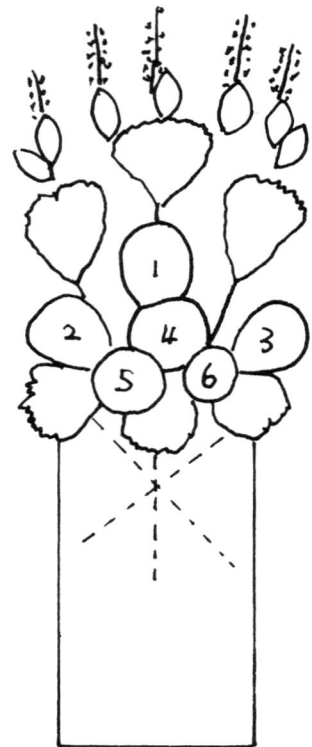

Filler flowers Take three bushy stems of nitens morrison. The tallest will be in front of the centre back piece of bookleaf. It should be approximately 4 cm (1½'') shorter than the bookleaf. The next stem of nitens morrison should be 6 cm (2½'') shorter than the first and will sit to the left of it while the remaining piece, also 6 cm (2½'') shorter than the first piece, will sit to the right of it. Cut three more pieces of nitens all about 12 cm (5'') long. Insert one at the centre front of the mouth of the vase, and one at either side, following the second diagram.

Feature flowers Start with the *Protea neriifolia*, numbered 1, 2 and 3 in the second diagram. Cut one stem (No. 1) to measure 14 cm (5½'') below the flower head. Insert this into the arrangement in front of the first stem of nitens morrison. Cut the two remaining protea stems (Nos 2 and 3) to measure 12 cm (5'') below the flower heads. Insert one into the left hand side of the arrangement and one to the right. Now cut all the banksia stems (Nos 4, 5 and 6) to measure 8 cm (3'') below the flower heads. Insert the first banksia

38

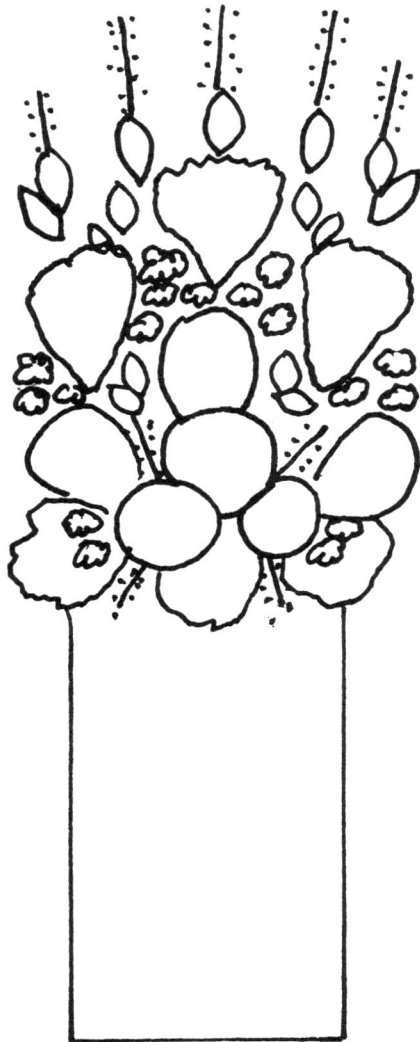

(No. 4) in front of the first protea but lower down. Insert the next two banksias (Nos 5 and 6), one to the left and one to the right of the first banksia, low down and grouped together. Cross the stems inside the vase.

Finishing off Distribute the ixodia evenly throughout the arrangement, keeping the tallest pieces for height behind the proteas and in front of the nitens morrison. Dot short pieces of stirlingia and bookleaf throughout the arrangement. Don't let the filling in overpower the flowers.

Proteas in a bark pot

Illustrated on page 47

Materials

bark pot 19 cm (7½'') diameter × 16 cm
   (6¼'') tall
half-block green or grey Oasis
Oasis pinholder complete with Oasis Fix
5 *Protea repens*
4 large dried pods of your choice
8 everlasting daisies
bunch tea-tree
one-third bunch bachelor buttons
one-third bunch narrow eucalypt leaves

Technique

Fixing base materials Press Oasis pinholder complete with Oasis Fix to centre bottom of the inside of the pot. Push Oasis onto pinholder with narrow side facing horizontally across the front.

Feature flowers Cut the first protea stem to measure 8 cm (3'') below the flower head. Insert this into the centre top of the Oasis. Cut the four remaining protea stems to measure 6 cm (2½'') below the flower head. Insert one in the centre of the left- and right-hand sides of the Oasis and one into the centre of the back and the front of the Oasis. A gentle curve should appear as you look across the tops of the proteas, as in the first diagram. Cut the pod stems to measure 7 cm (2¾'') and push a pod into each corner of the Oasis between the four outer proteas.

Outline Cut the tea-tree and insert pieces into the Oasis all over the arrangement between the proteas and pods, following the second diagram.

The tea-tree can be as tall as the proteas or it can extend just beyond them. Again the eye should be able to distinguish a gentle curve flowing from one side of the arrangement to the other.

Secondary flowers Dot the eight everlasting daisies throughout the arrangement. They should be lower than the proteas. The tallest everlasting daisies will be closest to the centre.

Filler flowers Use the bachelor buttons throughout the arrangement, distributing them evenly. Fill in any gaps revealing the Oasis with tea-tree and any left-over bachelor buttons. The tea-tree can be quite short.

Finishing off Cut pieces of eucalypt leaves and distribute evenly throughout, taking care that they do not overpower the arrangement.

7 WEDDING NOTES

Wide-brimmed wedding hat

Illustrated on page 48

Materials
light straw hat
sewing needle and thread
25 pussytails
one-third bunch oats
one-third bunch dried shivery grass
one-third bunch ixodia (South Australian daisy)
one-third bunch fine fern
half bunch German statice
3 metres (3¼ yards) fine bridal tulle

Technique

Fixing base materials   You will need approximately 10 clusters of flowers to encircle the hat, so divide all the floral material evenly into ten. Each cluster should be 11.5 cm (4½'') long, with the floral material staggered so that the grasses, ferns, oats and pussytails are the longest, then the German statice, with the ixodia lower down in the cluster.

Cut across stem ends evenly. Thread a needle with a long double thread and tie a knot at the end. Wind the knotted end around the base of the clustered stem for up to 5 cm (2''), pulling the thread tight with every turn. Leave a length of thread for sewing. Use the first diagram as a guide.

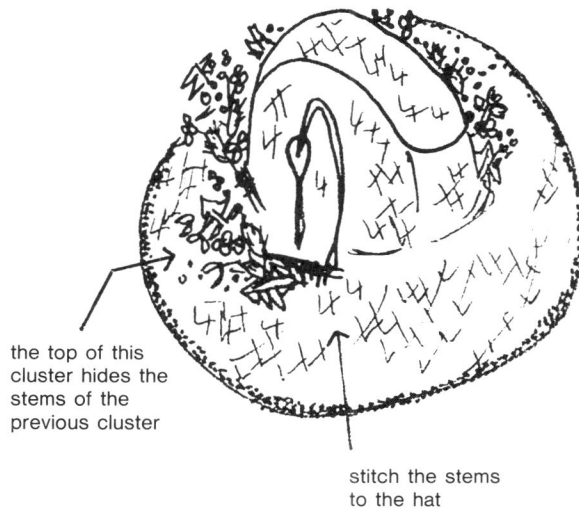

the top of this cluster hides the stems of the previous cluster

stitch the stems to the hat

Fixing flowers to hat   With the needle still attached, hold the cluster of flowers against the hat where the crown and brim meet. Push the needle through the hat on one side of the bound stem and bring it out on the other side. See second diagram. Continue to stitch the stem to the hat until it is secure. Position the next cluster against the hat so that the top of the cluster hides the stems of the first cluster. Continue around the hat, leaving a gap of about 8 cm (3'') at the back for the tulle bow.

Finishing off Cut a 70 cm (28'') wide strip from the length of tulle. Fold the strip in half lengthwise, making two 18 cm (7'') bow loops in the process and leaving trailing ends. Stitch the loops in the centre to form a proper bow, then stitch the bow into the space allowed at the back of the hat.

If you wish you can make another bow the same size but with shorter trailing ends and fasten it on top of the first bow.

Round wedding bouquet

Illustrated on page 48

Materials

1 metre (39'') fine bridal tulle
2 metres florist's tear ribbon
length 0.70 florist's wire
2 metres (2 ¼ yds) lace 6 cm (2 ½ '') wide
bunch German statice
one-quarter bunch pussytails
one-quarter bunch ixodia (South Australian daisy)
one-quarter bunch fine fern
one-quarter bunch shivery grass
one-quarter bunch oats

Technique

Fixing base materials   Use the bunch of German statice to form the base for the bouquet, organising it into a full circle in your hand.

Foliage   Insert the stems of fern evenly throughout the base of German statice. Then add the shivery grass and oats. All these stems will rise above the German statice, and must keep a round shape. Have all stems cross at one tying point, following the first diagram.

Filler flowers   Add the pussytails evenly through the arrangement, followed by the ixodia.

Finishing off   Wrap the florist's wire around the tying point at the stems and twist and secure. Cut away excess wire and cut the flower stems across 8 cm (3'') below the tying point. Wrap the tulle around the arrangement to cover stem ends and cut away excess. Take the lace and tie a standard bow around the tulle and the tying point of the bouquet. Leave trailing ends which can be cut on the cross.

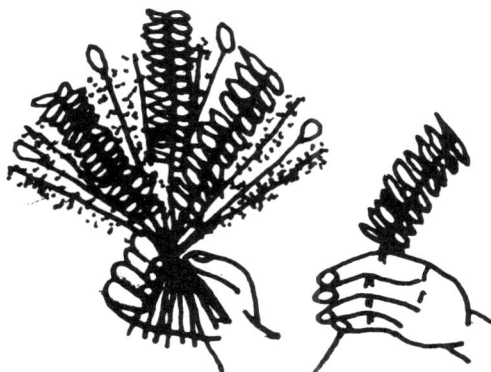

Tear florist's ribbon to a width of 2 cm (¾'') and make a 6-looped flower bow (see page 10). Leave long trailing ends which will be cut on the cross and curled with the blade of a pair of scissors or a sharp knife. Secure the bow with a thin piece of ribbon tied around the centre and around the tying point of the bouquet over the tulle and lace bow.

43

8 DRYING CUT FLOWERS AND FOLIAGES

All the arrangements outlined in the previous section were made with commercially available dried flowers. Some of these were dyed as well as dried.

For those of you without ready commercial access to dried flowers, or who wish to dry their own for fun, I have included this next section.

In this chapter I highlight the most commonly dried flowers and foliages, explaining the various methods employed to gain a professional finish. There are probably many other flowers and foliages with the potential for drying which remain undiscovered. I trust that this chapter will make you enthusiastic enough to do your own research and experiments.

insects cannot pollinate them—otherwise the seeds will drop. Pick hydrangeas when they begin to fade, just as the colour starts to turn.

Lavender should be picked just as the first florets open. Pick roses in bud or when the bud is just opening, and delphiniums before maturing, both for air drying.

You may want to trying something a little different. You could allow some of your flowers to go to seed and then collect the seed pods—alstroemeria is one to try, and so are the flower-like pods formed by onion and garlic plants. Try using spiky agapanthus heads after the florets have fallen off. All these make stunning accompaniments to arrangements.

When to pick

Pick flowers and foliages on a dry day, as soon as the dew has dried from the plant's surface. Because you wish these flowers and foliages to be preserved indefinitely, always pick perfect, unblemished material, preferably just before it reaches maturity. However, foliage that is to be glycerined should be mature, as young or dying foliage is inefficient at drawing up moisture. Helichrysums (everlasting daisies) should be picked in bud or with only one set of petals opened if you do not wish the centres to become exposed. Helichrysums keep developing even after they have been picked. If you do pick at a slightly more advanced stage, allow them to open inside where

Drying methods

A variety of drying methods is available. The choice is usually a matter of personal preference and experimentation, depending upon what plant species is being dried. The most commonly recognised method is air drying, in which plant material is hung upside down to dry, but it is definitely not the only way in which to dry flowers and foliages. Desiccants (drying agents) such as borax powder, silica gel or sand can be used. When supple foliage is the required result, then glycerine would be the choice. Other methods of preservation such as freeze drying, pressing leaves and flowers and even ironing ferns have their place. Let us have a look at these methods individually.

Pretty fridge magnet (page 32)

This topiary tree on a wooden board appears in high relief (page 30)

Wooden door hanger (page 33)

Terracotta pot picture in high relief (page 34)

Country style wreath (page 35)

Banksias and proteas arranged in a tall vase (page 38)

Proteas in a bark pot (page 40)

Banksias in a square terracotta pot (page 36)

Bridal flowers with a difference—see pages 41–43

Air drying

A wide variety of plant materials can be successfully air-dried. Most popular are seed pods, grasses and grains, berry branches, papery flowers, Australian and South African natives as well as some European flowers like delphiniums and rosebuds. More will be said about plant species later.

When you have chosen your material for drying, strip the stems of as many leaves as possible to speed up the process (unless of course you are drying for foliages) and tie stems together loosely in a bunch. Leave a tail of string long enough to tie over a hook or rafter. Make sure the room, shed or cupboard where these plant materials are to be dried is airy, and dark enough to preserve the colours of the plant materials. For this reason do not hang plant materials in direct sunlight.

Hanging flowers upside down in this manner allows the moisture contained naturally within the stem to run down towards the flower head; in most cases the stems of the dried product will become brittle. This is not always obvious in plants such as leptospermum (tea-tree), or in banksias or proteas, as they have naturally very woody stems, but as a general rule drying out of the stems will be an indication that the material has finished drying. Also remember as a guide that this method can take from 7 to 21 days, so it is a good idea to check your drying area regularly.

Some flowers will air-dry just as successfully in an upright position—flowers like banksias and proteas—but care must be taken that the stems are not bent over the edge of a container during the drying process. The stem can take on a curve in this situation rather than remaining straight.

Brittleness of the dried stems can become a problem with flowers which you may wish to later wire onto a false stem. Helichrysums (everlasting daisies) are one such example. Not only does the stem become brittle, but the flower head itself becomes hard, making it almost impossible to pass a wire through. Here's a tip.

From personal experience I have found the best method of wiring these flowers is not by the traditional hook method. Instead, while the flower is fresh cut away the stalk, leaving a 1.25 cm (½'') stub below the flower head. Take a wire, usually 0.71 mm (22 gauge), and push it up through the stub into the flower head. Make sure the wire end is not visible among the petals. As the flower dries it will shrink onto the wire making gluing unnecessary. I stand the wired helichrysums in groups in drinking glasses and store them in a dark cupboard until dried.

If flower heads become crushed or squashed during the air-drying process, they can generally be held over a steaming kettle to reverse the situation. Do not be surprised if during this you see the petals of flowers like helichrysums or ixodia (South Australian daisy) close up due to the moisture. Putting them out in the sun for up to an hour to dry off will cause the petals to reopen.

Thoroughly air-dried flowers and foliages can be stored either by leaving them hanging up or by wrapping individual bunches in butcher's paper and standing in a basket or other container. Dried material must be kept away from mice and the sun.

Grasses and seed pods can be sprayed with hairspray to keep them from falling.

Drying with desiccants

Desiccant is the term applied to a substance which withdraws moisture, e.g. silica gel, perlite aggregate, borax powder, sand. Plant materials can be buried in these and sealed in an airtight container. Over a period of time, which varies according to the type of plant being dried, preservation occurs. Most often the original colour of the flower or foliage is retained.

> **A health warning**
> Silica gel, perlite aggregate and other powders are hazardous to your health. Always wear a face mask when working with these materials to avoid inhalation.

Silica gel

Flowers like orchids, zinnias, dahlias, roses and bulb flowers respond well to silica gel. So does made-up work like corsages. Silica gel is popular because it dries materials quickly, usually within 48–72 hours. The disadvantages are that it is very expensive and can leave the flowers fragile. As with any other desiccant, make sure that the silica gel is 100% dry before use.

Silica gel is available from chemist shops. Make sure you buy the self-indicating sort. Fresh, dry and ready for use this gel is blue in colour. If it has turned pink, you will need to place it in a shallow tray and put it into an oven heated to 130°C (250°F) to dry out, when once again it will turn blue. Silica gel can be used over and over again by drying it out in this manner, but always remember to allow it to cool before use. Keep it stored in an airtight container.

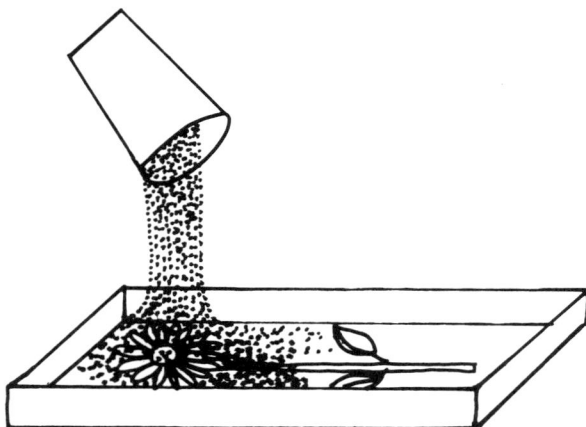

To dry flat-faced flowers such as daisies where you may wish to retain the flower's original stem, choose an airtight container in which you can fit a 'shelf'. Ths shelf can be made from materials such as polystyrene or even cardboard covered with foil. You must be able to poke holes in it large enough for the stems to pass through. The flower head will lie flat upon the shelf, and the stem will hang down through the hole in its natural position. See diagram.

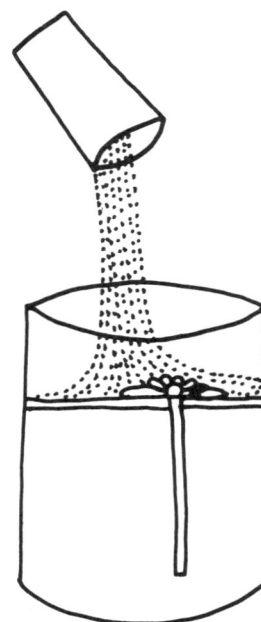

Pour the silica gel all over the flower you are drying, even under and between the petals, until the flower head is completely covered. Depending on the size of the container you may be able to dry several flowers at once. Seal the container and leave until dehydration has taken place.

If you do not wish to save the stems, pour about 2.5 cm (1'') of silica gel into the bottom of an airtight container (containers like biscuit and cake tins are good), place flower heads flat and face up on the gel so they are not touching each other, then cover the petals as before with more silica gel. Seal and store. Afterwards, if you wish to wire with a false stem, use 0.71 mm (22 gauge) wire and the hook method. Then cover with florist's tape (Parafilm).

Flowers like roses and bulb flowers can be dried on their sides. Place 2.5 cm (1'') of silica gel in the bottom of the container. Lay the flower on top lengthwise, then cover completely with silica gel. Seal and store.

Try something different! Pull the petals of a carnation out of the calyx and dry the calyx and stem to give a mini green tulip! Or pull the petals off some daisies and dry the fluffy centres and stems. These make unusual additions to a mix of dried flowers.

Since silica gel can be heavy, really delicate flowers may be better preserved using a borax powder or perlite aggregate.

Borax powder and perlite aggregate

Flowers which can be dried using silica gel can also be dried using borax powder and perlite aggregate but the drying time is longer.

Borax powder is available from hardware stores and some chemists. Perlite aggregate can be purchased from building suppliers.

Borax powder is a very finely textured powder, and you must make sure that all of the plant material is covered. It also has the habit of sticking to the surface of the dried material. Be prepared to spend a little time brushing powder away from the petals or leaves, using a small artist's brush, after you have removed dried material from the drying box.

The principle for drying materials with powders is the same as for drying with silica gel, except for the timing factor. Allow roughly 7–10 days (sometimes much longer). If unsure whether the plant material is ready, brush the desiccant aside, inspect and touch the petals. If crisp the procedure is finished. If the plant still feels 'alive', cover with powder again and reseal. Take another look a day or so later.

Borax can be used on its own, but if a heavier substance is needed mix two parts borax to one part clean sand. Mix perlite aggregate the same way.

Borax powder and perlite aggregate can be dried in the oven after use at 130°C (250°F) and stored in airtight containers.

Sometimes flowers dried with the lighter materials such as silica gel and borax look wrinkled. Try using a heavy material next time to 'iron' the petals.

Sand

Builder's sand can be used but it should be washed beforehand to remove any impurities. To wash, fill a bucket with sand to the three-quarter mark. Fill the bucket to the top with water. Stir the sand with your hand to dislodge any debris and allow the water to settle before scooping the debris off the surface. Do this several times with clean water until no more rubbish appears, and then dry the sand in a 130°C (250°F) oven for several hours. Put it through a sieve before using it.

Sand is very heavy so it is not suitable for really delicate flowers. Use it for roses, daisies, tulips and other medium weight flowers.

If the weather is warm, sand can be used uncovered. Flat-faced flowers like daisies can be placed face down on a tray filled with about 2.5 cm (1'') of sand, with their stalks sticking up as in the daigram. Other flowers, like roses, can be laid sideways on the sand. Cover with more sand, trickling it gently over the petals. Using a spoon, shake the spoonful of sand gently over the flower to be dried. Fill open-throated flowers like daffodils with sand.

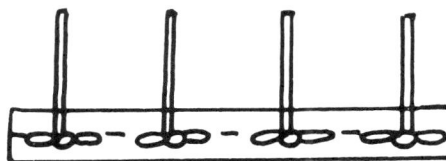

To avoid post-treatment shrivelling, make sure the flowers are completely dried before you remove them from the sand. The drying process may take at least 14 days. If in doubt, wipe some of the sand from the petals and feel them; if they are not dried replace the sand and wait a few more days before checking again.

Glycerine

Glycerine can be purchased from chemists. The usual dilution for plant work is one part glycerine to two parts boiling water. Stir the glycerine and water to mix thoroughly. This can be done in a saucepan on the stove. If you find this solution doesn't work, you may wish to try a stronger one, in which case one part glycerine to one part water is recommended.

Glycerining is the ideal method for preserving foliage and is rarely used on flowers, although *Thryptomene calycina* is an exception which comes to mind. Bracken fern and *Eucalyptus cinerea* (silver dollar gum), *Magnolia grandiflora* and ivy respond well. These and other glycerined foliages take on a supple and life-like appearance.

The procedure is relatively simple. Cut the stems of the plant to be treated on an angle under warm running water to remove any air embolism and then stand in about 10–15 cm (4''–6'') of solution. The solution can be used hot. Leave in a cool, dark, dry place until the leaves have absorbed the mixture and changed colour. You may need to top up the fluid level from time to time.

Remember, pick foliage in its prime for best results, neither too young nor too old. Autumn-toned leaves will drop, unfortunately, so don't use them.

Individual leaves, such as those of *Oreocallis wickhamii* (the North Queensland tree waratah) may be glycerined by placing the solution into a shallow dish and totally immersing the leaves until they have changed colour.

Glycerined leaves usually turn dark brown or grey. *Pittosporum rhombifolium* (diamond laurel) and the leaves of *Athertonia diversifolia* (blue almond tree) also respond well to glycerining. With investigation I am sure you will find much other foliage which will dry successfully. Whatever leaves you choose to treat by glycerining, once the colour change has occurred remove them from the tray, wash gently in clean water to remove any excess glycerine, and place them on blotting paper to dry.

Glycerining foliage or individual leaves can take anything from one week to ten, two to three weeks being the average. Again, the timing for different species varies. The actual texture of the plant material can also influence the timing. The thicker and firmer the leaf, the more time must be allowed.

If you wish to speed things up, you can wipe leaves individually with the solution before standing the stems in it.

Over-glycerining, when the leaves start to drip glycerine, can be a problem too. The best thing is to keep regular watch. When there is no longer a distinction between the leaves, you know the plant material is ready. Feel the undersides of the leaves. If they are slightly greasy to the touch, this too indicates it is time to remove the stems from the glycerine.

If you have left the material too long in the glycerine and the leaves are dripping, gently wipe off as much solution as possible and stand them in a dry place. Watch for mildew, which can be removed with soapy water.

If the glycerining process has obviously been completed but the leaves are crisp around the edges, hang the treated material upside down for a few days. This allows the glycerine solution in the plant to move to the tips of the leaves.

You can store leftover glycerine solution, but add approximately ¼–½ teaspoon of bleach to 500 ml (1 pint) of glycerine solution to discourage the formation of mildew.

Water drying

Some arrangements can be made using plant materials which will dry as they stand. That is, they will arrive in water-soaked Oasis or can be picked and placed in a vase containing about 5 cm (2'') of water. As the water evaporates so the material begins to dry. This happens particularly with arrangements using susceptible Australian native or South African plants. Some ferns and mature hydrangeas will also dry this way.

Tip: How to dry hydrangeas
The important factor in drying hydrangeas successfully lies in the picking. It is important to pick hydrangeas as they mature, that is, when the colour turns. Remove all but a few leaves. Cut and place in 2.5–5 cm (1''–2'') of water. Do not top the water level up but allow it to evaporate naturally. The hydrangeas should dry perfectly in this fashion. Hydrangeas can be air-dried or even glycerined, but water-drying is most consistently successful.

Microwave drying

Microwave drying flowers can be fun. A relatively modern way of drying flowers, it is still open to a lot of experimentation to determine just which flowers are suitable and how long they take to dry. Successful choices include carnations, daisies and daffodils. Trickier ones include magnolias and dahlias. Flower colours can change through microwaving although this is not always the case. Yellow flowers stay yellow while white flowers can take on a grey tinge and blue flowers can turn purple. Underdeveloped flowers dry more successfully than full blown ones, which can drop their petals.

There are two different techniques.

1. Put 5 cm (2'') of Kitty Litter into a microwave proof container. Place the flowers right side up on the Kitty Litter, spacing them evenly. The shortened flower stems are pushed down into the Kitty Litter so their petals aren't touching. Cover the petals completely with more Kitty Litter, which acts as a desiccant. Place one or more containers of flowers on the turntable, towards the centre. Place a cup of water on the edge of the turntable. Process on High for 30 seconds to three and a half minutes. While you are experimenting, start at the low end of the time scale. Leave the flowers covered with Kitty Litter in the container for 30 minutes after the microwave finishes as the drying process will continue. Check the flowers for dryness after that and return to the microwave for another couple of minutes if need be. Store dried flowers in an airtight container with a small amount of Kitty Litter with them to absorb any dampness.

2. Place 5 cm (2'') of silica gel in the bottom of a microwave proof container, poking the shortened flower stems into it. Cover the flower heads carefully with more silica gel crystals. Place half a cup of water in the microwave with the container and process on High for 2–4 minutes. Leave the flowers in the crystals overnight if possible. Store in an airtight container.

Freeze drying

Because of the expensive machinery involved freeze drying is only for the commercially minded. However, it is the latest technique in drying flowers and well worth a mention, if only for interest's sake.

Freeze drying flowers and foliages is a relatively new innovation, although freeze drying other products has been around for some time. This unique process dry-preserves 90% of all flowers giving them an extended life period of 6–12 months. However, when it comes to most foliages, according to the machine manufacturers glycerining gives a softer and more successful result. Freeze drying is the best of all the drying methods for maintaining the fresh look of most living blooms and presents a wonderful way to preserve bridal bouquets and other keepsakes.

Freeze drying works by first turning the water in plant materials into ice crystals; then, by a process of raising the temperature while at the same time lowering the atmospheric pressure, water is driven off the material's surface as vapour and extracted by a condensing process.

This is a simplification of a system which needs to be thoroughly studied. The manufacturer's explanation of the process is comprehensive and fairly easy to understand. Be advised though, that while freeze dried flowers are becoming widely popular in India, the USA, Japan and now Australia, machine prices can range from $50–70,000. For further information about freeze drying machines, contact Freeze Tec, Newmarket, Auckland, New Zealand or Dynavac, Wantirna South, Victoria, Australia.

Pressing

Drying flowers by pressing is both labour intensive and time consuming, because only small quantities can be done at a time, but the results are suitable for a lot of gift work. Some pressed flowers and foliages can take on a rather stiff appearance while others, like maidenhair fern, can look truly attractive. Pressed flowers and foliages used in gift lines such as flower pictures, greeting cards, collages and the like make most appealing novelties.

Choosing plant material

Flowers and foliages need to be pressed immediately after they have been picked, so have all your materials and tools ready (see next section).

Always pick plants in peak condition, as for the other preservation techniques. Make sure they are clean and dry. Blot away any dampness with blotting paper.

The greatest successes with pressed flowers are achieved with flowers which are flat, single-petalled, thin-tissued and open. Flowers like single roses, single delphiniums, pansies, forget-me-nots, violets, boronia and kangaroo paw make good subjects. Ferns, grasses and individual leaves provide the basis for interesting background material.

Flowers or foliages containing large amounts of water, e.g. succulents, are unsuitable, as are flowers with hard cores or rigid petals. Clusters of flowers can be separated from their stems, while some large flowers can have their petals removed to be used individually. Any stalks pressed should be as fine as possible, and can be gently curved into shape by the use of sticky tape. If you are using larger stalks, make sure they are soft enough to press.

How to press

Flower presses can be used if you wish, but an inexpensive method of pressing flowers and foliages is to place them between the pages of a heavy book. That's where old telephone directories come into play. The beauty of them is that if any staining of the pages occurs, it doesn't matter.

Lay the flowers and other plant material flat on a sheet of blotting paper or tissue paper. Make sure that none of the petals or pieces overlap or touch each other. If petals do overlap, slide a piece of tissue paper between them. To avoid handling and potentially damaging fragile material, arrange the pieces on the paper with the aid of a small paint or makeup brush. Cover with another piece of paper so that the flowers are sandwiched.

Place between the back pages of a telephone book. Work from back to front of the book so you don't disturb the previous layers. Cut tags and label the pages with the names of the material being pressed, e.g. kangaroo paws, pansies, ferns, flannel flowers. Make the tags extend beyond the page so each section is identifiable at a glance.

Weight is an important factor in the success of pressing flowers, so you may need to pile more books on top of the pressing book.

If using a flower press do up the wing nuts gently for the first 10 days or so to allow the material to settle. Tighten the nuts more securely during the following few weeks.

Flowers can be pressed for periods ranging from three months to a year. The longer the plant material is pressed the thinner it becomes, so the choice is up to you.

To avoid mould and to aid in dehydration, press flowers in a dry area with good airflow.

To help retain the colour of pressed flowers and foliages, when the pressing time is up remove them from the press, lift the top layer of paper and sprinkle lightly with borax powder. Cover them again with the sheet of paper and place in an airtight container, making sure to keep the plant materials flat. Store for another few weeks before using.

Pressing ferns with a steam iron

Some ferns can be dried successfully by pressing with a hot iron, in particular maidenhair fern. Place the fern between two sheets of waxed paper (sandwich wrap), making sure the waxed side is lying against the fern, and cover the top layer of paper with a cloth. Fill an iron with water, set it on Wool heat and iron for up to five minutes, lifting the paper every so often to release any build-up of steam. The end result should be a shiny green fern which will retain its colour for a long period.

Blotting paper can be used instead of wax paper, but colour changes may occur.

This method could be tried for other fine ferns such as *Sticherus lobatus* (umbrella fern) or *Bowenia serrulata* (Byfield fern).

9 GETTING STARTED

In this section I have prepared lists for the enthusiastic, covering the commonly used methods for preserving cut flowers and foliages and the species which would seem suitable for each method. Some plants have been included because of the successful preservation of similar types or species, even though their particular drying potential is unknown. These are lists to which you will no doubt wish to add.

Suggested plants for air drying

Acacia (Wattle, esp. *Acacia macredenia*)
Achillea (Yarrow)
Acrolinium (Rose Everlasting Daisy)
Actinodium cunninghamii (Albany Daisy)
Allium (garlic, leeks and onion flower heads)
Anigozanthos species (Kangaroo Paw)
Banksia species
Barley
Beaufortia decussata
Beaufortia sparsa
Celosia (Cockscomb)
Chrysanthemum parthenium (Button Chrysanthemum)
Conospermum (Smoke Bush)
Craspedia (Billy Buttons)
Cytisus (Broom)
Delphinium (Larkspur)
Dillwynia retorta (Eggs and Bacon)
Dipsacus (Teasel)
Dryandra formosa (Showy Dryandra)
Dryandra praemorsa (Cut-leaf Dryandra)
Eucalyptus
Grevillea hookeriana
Grasses
Gypsophila, esp. 'Bristol Fairy' (Baby's Breath)
Helichrysum species (Everlasting Daisies/Paper Daisies/Strawflowers)
Helipterum species (Everlasting Daisies/Paper Daisies)

Hydrangea
Hypocalymma puniceum
Isopogon species (Drumsticks)
Ixodia achillioides (South Australian Daisy)
Lachnostachys (Lambstails)
Lavender
Leucadendron
Liatris (Gay Feather)
Limonium 'Misty' (pink, white, blue)
Limonium 'Oceanic' (pink, white, blue)
Limonium sinuata (Statice)
Lunaria annua (Honesty)
Melaleuca acuminata
Melaleuca heugelii
Molucella laevis (Bells of Ireland)
Oats
Protea
Ptilotus (Mulla Mulla, incl. 'pussytails')
Roses (preferably rosebuds)
Rumex (Dock)
Salix caprea (Pussy Willow)
Serruria florida (Protea family) 'Blushing Bride' and 'Sugar 'n Spice'
Solidago (Goldenrod)
Verticordia species
Waitzia acuminata (Everlasting Daisy)
Wheat

Suggested plants for drying with desiccants

Actinotus helianthus and A. superbus (Flannel Flower)
Agapanthus (individual florets)
Blandfordia grandiflora (Christmas Bells)
Bowenia serrulata (Byfield Fern)
Brachycome iberidifolia (Swan River Daisy)
Brunonia australis (Blue Pincushion)
Carnations
Castanospermum australe (Black Bean Flowers)
Ceratopetalum gummiferum (NSW Christmas Bush)
Clianthus formosa (Sturt's Desert Pea)
Cochlospermum gillivraei (Kapok Bush)
Crinum pedunculatum (River Lily)
Dahlias
Dampiera species
Dianthus
Eriostemon species (Waxflower)
Freesias
Glossodia
Gompholobium (Pea family)
Hibbertia
Iris

Lechenaultia
Lilium longiflorum (Christmas Lily)
Linum marginale
Marguerite (Daisy)
Melastoma denticulatum
Narcissus (Daffodil and Jonquil)
Nigella (Love-in-a-Mist)
Orchids
Ornithogalum
Paeonia (Peony—flower)
Rhododendron
Roses
Scabiosa (Pincushion)
Sphaerolobium macranthus
Sweet Peas
Tagetes (Marigold)
Thysanotus multiflorus (Fringed Lily)
Tulip
Typhonium brownii (dark purple arum-like lily)
Violets
Xyris
Zantedeschia (Calla Lily)

Suggested plants for glycerining

Adiantum (Maidenhair Fern)
Aspidistra
Athertonia diversifolia (Blue Almond Tree—foliage)
Betula pendula (Silver Birch)
Brassaia actinophylla (Umbrella Tree—foliage)
Daviesia cordata (Bookleaf)
Eucalyptus (esp. E. cinerea 'Spinning Gum')
Gladioli (foliage)
Grevillea (foliage)
Gypsophila (esp. 'Bristol Fairy')
Hedera (Ivy)
Helichrysum diosmifolium (Wild Rice/Sago Bush)

Hydrangea
Iris (foliage)
Lauris nobilis (Bay Laurel)
Magnolia grandiflora (foliage)
Molucella laevis (Bells of Ireland)
Oreocallis wickhamii (North Queensland Tree Waratah—foliage)
Pittosporum (Diamond Laurel)
Pteridium esculentum (Bracken Fern)
Solidago (Goldenrod)
Sticherus lobatus (Umbrella Fern)
Thryptomene calycina

Suggested plants for pressing

Acacia (Wattle)
Actinotus helianthi and *A. superbus* (Flannel Flower)
Actinodium cunninghamii (Albany Daisy)
Adiantum (Maidenhair Fern)
Anigozanthos species (Kangaroo Paw)
Bauera rubioides (Pink Dog Rose)
Bowenia serrulata (Byfield Fern)
Brachycome species (Australian Daisy)
Ceratopetalum gummiferum (NSW Christmas Bush)
Clianthus formosa (Sturt's Desert Pea)
Dampiera species (five-petalled, blue fan-shaped flowers)
Darwinia species
Daviesia cordata (Bookleaf)
Delphinium (Larkspur)
Epacris species (Common Heath—can press individual bells)
Eucalyptus
Gladioli (individual flowers)
Grasses
Hedera (Ivy)
Helichrysum species (Everlasting Daisies/Paper Daisies/Strawflowers)

Helipterum species (Everlasting Daisies/Paper Daisies)
Hibbertia species (brilliant yellow and orange flowers)
Iris
Lunaria annua (Honesty)
Marguerite (Daisy)
Melaleuca species
Monotoca species (individual bells)
Myosotis alpestris (Forget-me-not)
Paeonia (Peony—foliage)
Pansies
Papaver (Poppy)
Patersonia sericea (Native Iris)
Pimelea linifolia 'Pink Form' (Button Flower)
Pteridium esculentum (Bracken Fern)
Ptilotus species (Mulla Mulla, incl. 'pussy tails')
Sticherus lobatum (Umbrella Fern)
Violas
Violets
Waitzia (Everlasting Daisies)

10 AUSTRALIAN AND EXOTIC FLOWERS AND FOLIAGES

Key:

Feature flower   The main flower in an arrangement

Secondary flower   The second most important flower in an arrangement

Filler flower   Fills in between other flowers and foliages

Outline flower   Used for making the outline of the arrangement

Exotics

Allium (Flowering Onion)

Beaded white-flowering balls are borne on long straight stems. Filler or feature flower. Flowering time late spring/early summer. Stalk length approximately 30 cm (12''). Dry by air drying.

Allium

Anemone

A bulb plant producing a wide selection of flower colours including red, blue, rose and white. Flowers are distinguished by a black centre and are available as doubles or singles. Secondary flower. Flowering time spring. Stalk length approximately 30 cm (12''). Dry using silica gel.

Antirrhinum (Snapdragon)

Tall straight spikes with clustered flower heads up the stem. Many colours ranging from whites, mauves, pinks through to reds and yellow. Good outline flower. Flowering time spring/summer. Stalk length varies to approximately 30–40 cm (12–16''). Dry using silica gel.

Aster

Daisy-like flowers are borne on tall stems. Come in singles or doubles. Colours include white, pink, red, yellow, blue, maroon and apricot. Secondary flower. Flowering time summer/early autumn. Stalk length approximately 30 cm (12''). Dry using silica gel.

Calendula 'Pacific Giant'

Large flat-faced orange or yellow blooms. Secondary flower. Flowering time winter/spring. Stalk length 35 cm (14''). Dry using silica gel.

Centaurea cyanis (Cornflower)
Flower heads are approximately the size of a 10 cent coin atop a straight stem. Flowers are pink, white and rich blue, the blue being the most renowned. Good secondary flower. Flowering time spring/summer. Stalk length approximately 30 cm (12''). Air dry.

Dahlia
Come in pompom form and semi-doubles. Colours pink, orange, yellow and white. Make good secondary or feature flowers. Flowering time late summer to early autumn. Stalk length approximately 30 cm (12''). Dry using silica gel or sand.

Dahlias—clockwise from top: cactus, dwarf marchionette, nymphea and pompom types

Delphinium (Larkspur)
Tall spikes of clustered rich blue, lilac, pink or mauve flowers. Good outline flower. Flowering time late spring/summer. Stalk length over 40 cm (16''). Dry by air drying.

Dianthus (Carnations)
Come in a variety of types including micro, spray, field and sims or standard. Available in up to 19 different colours depending on type. Stalk length over 30 cm (12''). Feature or secondary flower. Flowering time all year. Dry using silica gel.

Digitalis (Foxglove)
Dry for seed pods. Flowering time spring. Collect the seedheads at the end of the season and rub the dead flower petals off to reveal the seed pods. Secondary flower. Stalk length over 40 cm (16''). Dry by air drying.

Erica (Heath)
Usually flowerheads look as though there are beads dotted on the foliage. Flower colours include cream, pink, mauve and green. Great filler flower. Flowering time autumn/spring. Stalk length 30 cm (12'') plus. Air dry.

Gypsophila
This plant produces fine sprays of the tiniest white flowers like dots on fine branching stems. Use as filler flower. Flowers are produced abundantly during spring/autumn, otherwise all year. Either air dry or glycerine. Glycerine will turn flower stalks a creamy brown.

Hydrangea
These large balls of open florets come in white, blue or pink. Blue is produced by acid soil, pink by lime soil. Feature or filler flower. Flowering time spring. Stalk length 30 cm (12''). Dry by air drying, leaving in 5 cm (2'') of water or by glycerining.

Lathyrus odoratus (Sweet Pea)
Highly fragrant pea flowers in a variety of colours ranging from lilac and blue to rose pink and white. Filler flower. Flowering time is spring. Stalk length approximately 20–30 cm (8''–12''). Dry using silica gel.

Spray carnation

Lavandula (Lavender)
Different varieties including French, English and Spanish. Lovely filler flower. Flowering time is mainly winter/spring but sometimes continues into summer. Stalk length approximately 20 cm (8''). Air dry.

Limonium (Annual Statice)
Tufts of papery flowers are borne on long branching stems. Flower colours include blue, violet, white, yellow, apricot and rose. Filler flower. Flowering time spring/summer. Stalk length approximately 60 cm (24''). Can be air dried.

Limonium—Statice and Fairy Statice

Limonium (hybrids 'Misty' and 'Oceanic')
Fine branching stems displaying blue, pink (not 'Oceanic') or white flowers. A filler flower often used in place of gypsophila. Flowering time late winter/spring/summer. Stalk length approximately 60 cm (24''). Air dry.

Molucella laevis (Bells of Ireland)
Green erect stems display clusters of green bell-like 'flowers' along their length. Good outline flower. Flowering time spring. Stalk length 30–60 cm (12''–24''). Air dry or use glycerine.

Narcissus (Jonquils and Daffodils)
Come in a variety of colours from creamy white to yellow and orange. Bulb flower which is produced in spring. Stalk length approximately 30 cm (12''). Feature or secondary flower. Dry using silica gel or sand. Can try microwaving.

Lavender

Paeonia officinalis (Paeony Rose)
Varying shades of pink and white flowers with pink streaks. A lovely fragrant large flower. Good feature flower. Flowering time spring/summer. Stalk length approximately 30 cm (12''). Dry using silica gel or sand.

Papaver (Poppy)
Unfortunately the flower petals cannot be preserved except by pressing but the seed pods can. Allow the pods to dry outdoors, then remove the spent petals and foliage and hang upside down to air dry. Filler flower. Stalk length 30 cm (12'')

Rosa (Roses)
Come in a magnificent array of colours and varieties. Feature flowers. Flowering time spring/summer/autumn. Stalk length varies, to 60 cm (24''). Dry using silica gel or sand. Can try air drying tight buds.

Tulipa (Tulip)
Comes in a variety of colours including scarlet, golden yellow, white, pink and red. A bulb flower which makes a good feature flower. Flowering time spring. Stalk length 30 cm (12'') plus. Dry using silica gel or sand.

Zinnia
Comes in a variety of types including doubles, semi-doubles and twisted petals. Feature or secondary flower. Available in mixture of colours including yellow, orange, purple, red and white. Flowering time late summer to early autumn. Stalk length approximately 30 cm (12''). Dry using silica gel or sand.

East coast and inland Australian natives

Acacia
Best suited to drying is *Acacia macredenia* (zig-zag wattle). Filler flower. Acacias flower winter to spring. Air dry.

Anigozanthos (Kangaroo Paw)
Stems vary in length from 40 cm (16'') to over 60 cm (24''). Comes in a wide range of colours including green, yellow, orange and red. Outline flower or filler. Depending on species flowers summer/spring or late winter to summer. Air dry.

Banksia
Several different banksias to choose from, including *B. ericifolia, B. 'Giant Candles'* and *B. robur*. Flowering time autumn/winter/summer. Feature flower. Air dry.

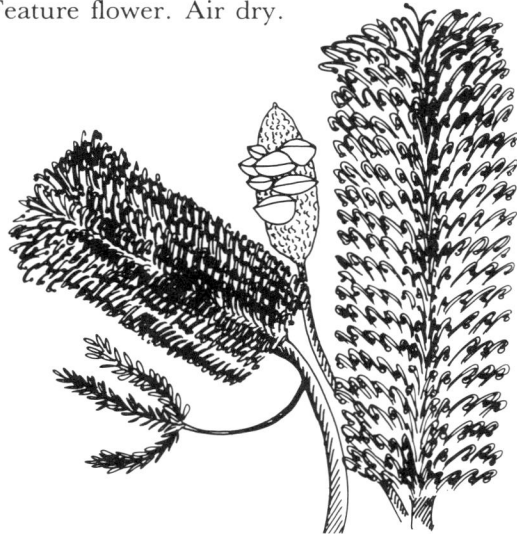

Banksia ericifolia on the left, *Banksia* 'Giant Candles' on the right

Banksia robur (Swamp Banksia)

Dodonaea (Hop Bush)
Seed capsules are the thing to dry here. They appear in summer. Stalk length approximately 60 cm (24''). Filler flower. Air dry.

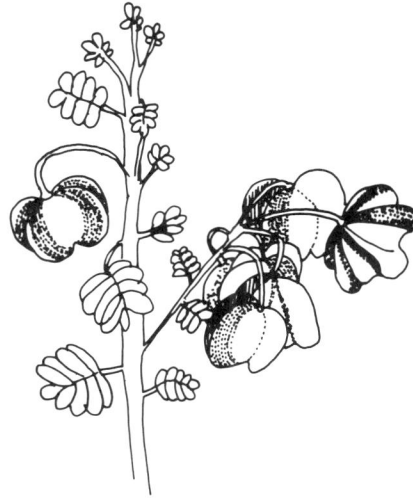

Dodonea pinnata (Hop Bush)

Helichrysum bracteatum

Helichrysum (Paper Daisy/Strawflower/ Everlasting Daisy)
Come in a wide variety of colours, from deep red to pink, cream and yellow. Pick when first or second row of petals have turned down for best results. Flowering time spring. Stalk length approximately 30 cm (12'') but these flowers are usually wired. Secondary or filler flower. Air dry.

Helipterum (Everlasting Daisy/Paper Daisy)
Pink or white, flat, open flower, usually with a distinctive black ring around the centre of the

inner petals. Secondary flower. Flowering time spring. Stalk length approximately 30 cm (12''). Air dry.

Ixodia achillioides (South Australian or Mountain Daisy)
This plant displays clusters of tiny white flowers which are easy to dye. Filler flower. Flowering time summer. Stalk length approximately 40–60 cm (16''–24''). Air dry.

Stirlingia
Masses of fluffy small grey 'balls' are borne along the stems. Also used in bud form. Outline material or filler flower. Flowering time summer. Stalk length 60 cm (24''). Air dry.

Telopea speciosissima (Waratah)
The waratah is a well known and popular cut flower, valued for its large, rich red flowers. It isn't often dried as it shrinks and browns but it can still be rather attractive. Other varities for different areas are *T. oreades* (Gippsland waratah) and *T. truncata* (Tasmanian waratah). Feature flower. Flowering time spring. Stalk length approximately 60 cm (24''). Air dry.

Telopea speciosissima (NSW Waratah)

Thryptomene calycina

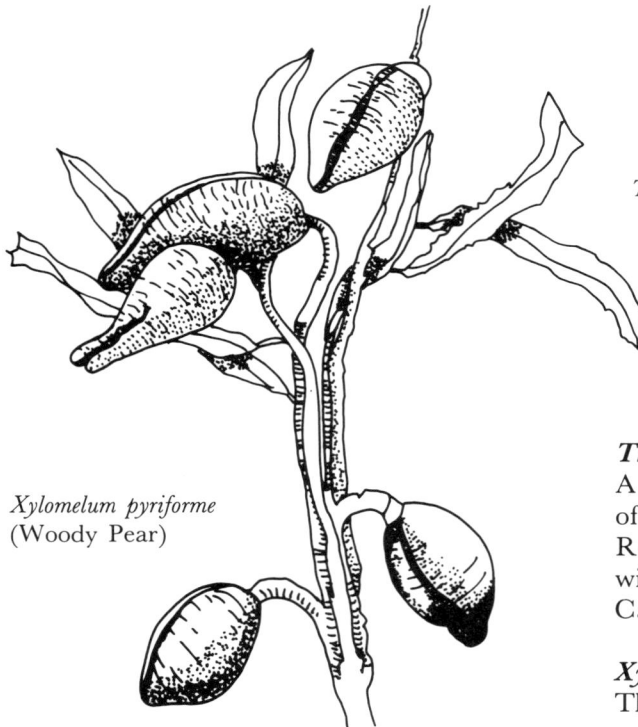

Xylomelum pyriforme (Woody Pear)

Thryptomene calycina
A popular cut flower with fine foliage and masses of tiny pink open flowers and pink buds. Renowned as a filler flower. Flowering time winter. Stalk length approximately 60 cm (24''). Can be dried using glycerine.

Xylomelum pyriforme (Woody Pear)
This plant is grown for its pear-shaped nuts. Nuts are everlasting but should be stored carefully as they can become mildewed. Flowers appear during spring, later followed by the nuts. Stalk length up to 60 cm (24''). Air dry.

Western Australian natives

Anigozanthos (Kangaroo Paw)

Many different varieties from 60 cm in length to 1 m (24''–39''). Red, green and yellow are most common colours. Outline or filler flower. Flowering time spring/summer. Air dry.

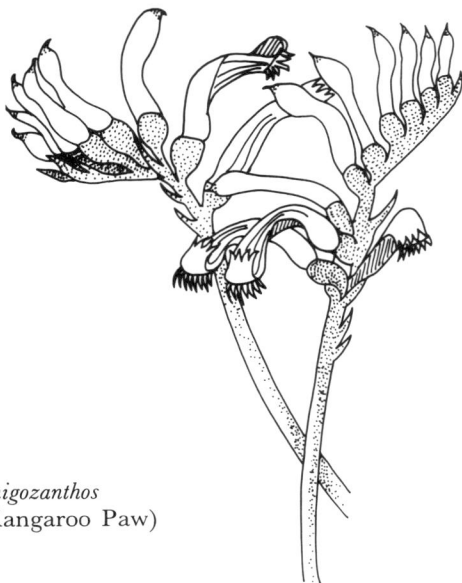

Anigozanthos
(Kangaroo Paw)

Banksia

A large variety, including *B. baxterii, B. burdettii, B. coccinea, B. hookeriana, B. media, B. menziesii, B. prionotes, B. speciosa.* Colours range from cream to red and grey striped to mauve. Autumn to spring flowering depending on species. Feature flowers. Air dry.

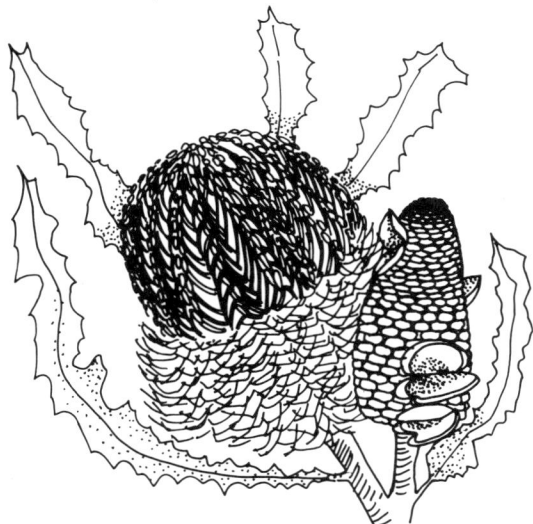

From left to right: *Banksia coccinea, B. hookeriana, B. baxterii*

Beaufortia sparsa

Stiff green branches bear small brilliant orange-red bottlebrush flowers which are popular in both fresh and dried arrangements. Flowering time summer/autumn. Stalk length approximately 60 cm (24''). Air dry.

Conospermum stoechadis (Smoke Bush)

This small erect shrub produces flowers which are blue-grey shaggy, woolly wisps. Filler flower. Flowering time spring/summer. Stalk length around 60 cm (24''). Air dry.

Banksia menziesii

Conospermum stoechadis (Smoke Bush)

Craspedia uniflora (**Billy Buttons**)
This unusual member of the daisy family has leaves low to the ground from which flowers or 'buttons' appear on long spikes. The flower heads can be quite substantial, approximately the diameter of a 10 cent coin. Filler flower. Flowering time spring/summer. Stalk length up to 45 cm (18''). Air dry.

Dryandra
D. formosa has finely serrated rich green leaves and golden-rust rosette flowers or brushes. The flower heads are approximately 6 cm (2½'') in diameter and the stems are long and fine. Perfect for use as filler or secondary flower. Flowering time spring to early summer. Stalk length approximately 60 cm (24''). While *D. praemorsa* produces yellow-green brushes similar in size to *D. formosa* the flowers have a slightly heavier appearance. Good as secondary or filler flower. Flowering time spring. Stalk length over 30 cm (12''). Both dryandras are air dried.

Dryandra praemorsa (Cut-leaf Dryandra) on the left, with *D. formosa* (Showy Dryandra) on the right

Lachnostachys eriobotrya (**Lambs' Tails**)
Grey woolly foliage and white cotton-wool type clumps of flowers. An unusual filler flower. Flowering time spring. Stalk length approximately 60 cm (24''). Air dry.

On the left, *Verticordia nitens* 'Morrison', on the right *V. brownii*

Verticordia
Many different types producing masses of tiny woolly flower heads. *V. brownii* (cauliflower morrison) and *V. nitens* (golden nitens) perhaps best known. Filler flower. Flowering time summer. Stalk length approximately 60 cm (24''). Air dry.

Xylomelum angustifolium (**Woody Pear**)
A tree valued in the cut flower industry for its pear-shaped nuts. Nuts are everlasting but should be stored carefully as they can become mildewed. Flowers appear during summer, followed by nuts. Stalk length up to 60 cm (24''). Air dry.

Tasmanian native plants

Banksia marginata (**Honeysuckle Banksia**)
The brushes are cream to greeny-yellow coloured and well formed. Use as feature flower. Stems approximately 30 cm (12''). Air dry.

Epacris impressa (**Heath**)
This plant displays bell-like flowers in white, pink and red. Filler flower. Flowering time autumn

to summer. Stalk length 30 cm (12''). Air dry but flowers shrink.

Helichrysum scorpioides (**Scorpion Everlasting Daisy/Strawflower**)
Bright yellow daisies for use fresh or dried. Small secondary flower. Flowering time spring/summer. Stalk length 30 cm (12''). Wire stems and air dry.

South African native plants

Leucadendron

A multitude of varieties here, including plants used for their cones rather than their flowers such as *L. conicum*. Lovely flowers produced by *L. laureolum* and *L.* 'Silvan Red'. Secondary or feature flower. Depending on variety autumn/ winter spring flowering. Air dry.

Protea

Most popular is *P. cynaroides* (King Protea) which has flower heads as large as a saucer. Flowering time is winter/spring. Feature flowers. Also *P. magnifica* (Queen Protea), flowering time late winter/summer, and *P. neriifolia* or *P.* 'Pink Ice'. All make excellent feature flowers but tend to brown when dried. Air dry. In all cases flower petals can be pulled off to expose attractive cones.

Leucadendron eucalyptifolium, a small-leaf flowered variety

Clockwise from top right: *Protea longiflora* (flower and bud), *P. repens* (fully open) and two views of *P. neriifolia*

Leucodendron sessile, with the male flower on the left, the female on the right

Protea cynaroides

Orchids

Cattleyas, cymbidiums, dendrobiums and others can be successfully dried using silica gel.

Cymbidium Peter Pan 'Greensleeves'

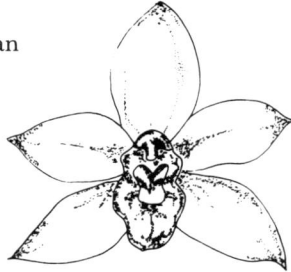

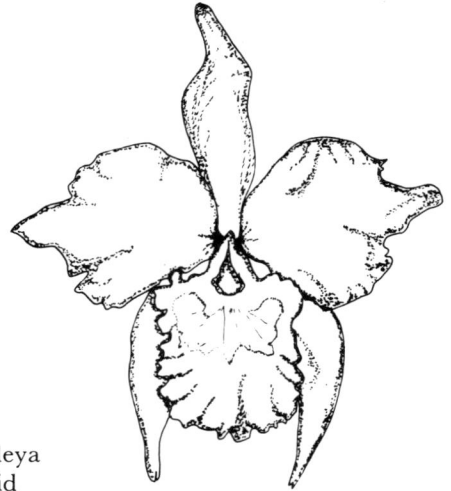

Cattleya
orchid

Foliages and ferns

Adenanthos obovata (Basket Fern)
Long, thin, shapely single branches with tiny oval green leaves covering the stem. Wonderful as outline material or for filling in between flowers. When dried changes colour gradually to a deep rich brown. Air dry.

Adiantum (Maidenhair Fern)
Pretty fine scalloped foliage is ideal for bouquets and other wedding work as well as for general use. Iron dry using wax paper.

Asparagus plumosa
Dainty-leaved long trailing fern frequently used in wedding work and for large, flowing pedestal arrangements. Air dry.

Aspidistra
Long, firm, tapering, shiny green leaves. Air dry or glycerine.

Athertonia diversifolia (Blue Almond Tree)
Large, glossy, dark green leaves measuring up to 15 cm × 7.5 cm (6'' × 3''). Useful in modern floristry. Leaves eventually turn rich chocolate brown before crinkling. Can be glycerined.

Buxus (Box)
Masses of tiny rounded leaves. Air dry.

Cycas media
Large, stiff, dark green palm leaves. Air dry.

Daviesia cordata (Bookleaf)
Small to medium-sized broad, tapering leaves which are gum-like in appearance bearing leafy seed pods. Can be air dried or glycerined.

Daviesia cordata (Bookleaf)

Eremophila
Tall straight single stems are covered in masses of long narrow leaves. Great as outline material or where interesting texture is required. Air dry.

Eucalyptus
A large variety which includes tapering koala bear-like foliage as well as rounded leaf versions like *E. cinerea* and *E. perriniana*. Air dry or glycerine.

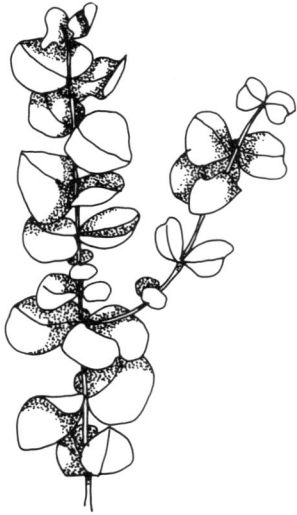

Eucalyptus cinerea (Spinning Gum)

Grevillea hookeriana
Long serrated leaves and long straight stems. Foliage dries to a pretty brown colour. Air dry.

Lauris nobilis (Bay Laurel)
Lovely shaped leaves which can be glycerined.

Leucadendron
A wide variety can be used as everlasting foliage before cones and flowers form. Try *L. argenteum*, *L. conicum* and *L. laureolum*, just to name a few. Air dry.

Lycopodium
Dainty fern-like leaves, most popular being *L. myrtifolium* (long club moss or mountain moss) and *L. phlegmaria* (coarse or common tassel fern). Air dry.

Magnolia grandiflora (Evergreen Magnolia)
Large leaves can be glycerined.

Ptostrata (Scrub Leaves)
Extremely attractive finely-toothed medium sized leaves. Outstanding feature leaves. Can be air dried.

Left and centre: *Lycopodium phlegmaria* (Coarse Tassel Fern); on the right *L. phlegmarioides* (Layered Tassel Fern)

Salix caprea (Pussy Willow)
Slender brown stems display buds in winter which can be stripped to reveal fluffy white interiors.

Salix matsudana (Tortured Willow)
Twisting bare branches in winter. Air dry.

Sasa fortunei (Dwarf Bamboo)
Small growing bamboo. Air dry.

Templetonia
Lovely upright tall single stems, sometimes branching out into stem clusters at the top. Air dry.

Xanthorrhoea
Lovely sprays of slender long grass-like stems. Great for adding height or curling. Air dry.

APPENDIX— BLEACHING AND DYEING

Not all plant material looks as interesting dried as it does alive. Contrast and excitement can be added to dried arrangements by the judicious use of bleached or dyed material. A number of the arrangements in this book include materials treated in these ways.

Bleaching

A process for the enthusiast to experiment with. Try bleaching wild oats, wheat, thistle, ferns, eucalyptus leaves, hydrangeas and any other plants you want to try after they have dried.

Some plant materials will need full strength bleach, some a mixture of 50% bleach to 50% water. The actual bleaching time can be anywhere from 15 minutes to one day, depending upon what material you are working with. Over-bleaching can weaken petals, stems and foliage. Use a plastic container.

When the colour of the plant material has been bleached out, rinse it in cold water and hang up in an airy place to dry. Keep away from sunlight, which may have a yellowing effect. It is especially important to remove all traces of bleach or sulphur dioxide if you are planning to dye the bleached flowers or foliages.

Bleaching is not a prerequisite for dyeing, but may be necessary if you wish to dye dark coloured plant material a lighter shade.

Dyeing

Spray dyes

The fastest method of dyeing plant material, either living or dried, is to use aerosol canned dyes such as Designmaster, a product sold through florist's suppliers and some flower markets. When using such products avoid inhalation of the dye as well as skin contact in case of toxicity. The colour range is huge and the finished effect is most attractive. Drying time for dyed materials is about 10–15 minutes.

Textile dyes

The plant materials most commonly dyed are dried wildflowers, foliages and grasses. Dyes used are usually those designed for textiles. In the past food dyes have been used, but while relatively safe to handle the range of colours is limited and they aren't always lightfast. Food dyes can also be more expensive than other dyes because of the thoroughness of the costly toxicity testing required for food additives.

Of the textile dyes, those designed for dyeing acrylic fibres tend to give the best results. These are known as 'basic dyes'. Small amounts can be purchased at most chemists in a wide range of colours. For commercial dyers 5 kg lots and over can be purchased through chemical companies like Ciba-Geigy in Melbourne.

Follow the manufacturer's directions for the ratio of water to dye. Gloves and dust masks should be worn when weighing out the powder. If possible, the water should be boiling. Use a large tub or bath. Dip dye the plant material in the dye solution, stirring the dye throughout the process to maintain evenness of colour. Use rubber gloves and, if possible, squeeze out excess solution.

Stand plant material upright in plastic buckets or other non-corrosive containers to dry, or lay it on plastic meshing in airy surroundings, out of direct sunlight which will fade the dye. To avoid colour contamination make sure that different plant materials and colours aren't touching.

Absorption dyes

This form of dyeing requires living plant material to be stood in the dye solution. As the plant drinks, so it absorbs the dye and becomes coloured. Mostly used for light coloured plants, this method can also be used to highlight veins in darker plant material, using bright colours like red. Many absorption dyes can be added to the glycerining process.

Absorption dyeing is very much a trial and error procedure, as not all plants give good colouring results. For the best effect use freshly picked, good quality flowers or foliages which have a fast water usage rate. Recut stems on an angle under water before placing in the dye solution. This removes any air blockages and means the plant stems won't be sitting flat on the base of the container.

Follow manufacturer's directions for making up the solution. The warmer the dye solution the better the results will be. Dye seems to be absorbed into the stems more readily with heat, so warm the solution to somewhere between 30°–40°C (85°–104°F).

Cotton dyes can be tried but best results appear to be obtained by using food dyes. One supplier is the company Robert Bryce in Melbourne.

Index